COOKERY INTERNATIONAL

FISH
MAIN COURSES

COOKERY INTERNATIONAL

FISH
MAIN COURSES

Galley Press

© 1985 Orbis Verlag
English language edition designed and produced by
Autumn Publishing Limited, 10 Eastgate Square,
Chichester, England.

Translation by Meckie Hellary
Editorial by Sherian Morgan
              Rosemary Blott

Published in this edition by Galley Press, an imprint
of W H Smith & Son Limited
Registered No 237811 England.
Trading as WHS Distributors, St John's House,
East Street, Leicester, LE1 6NE

Typeset by Avonset, Midsomer Norton, Bath, England.

Printed in Italy by GEA, Milan,
in association with Keats European Ltd.

ISBN 0–86136–697–2

Exact conversion to metric from imperial (28.35) does not
always give convenient working quantities. Therefore
metric quantities have been given in units of the nearest
25 grams, except where a different amount is necessary
to produce a balanced recipe.
Do be careful to follow 1 type of measure throughout the
recipe.
All recipes are for four people unless otherwise stated.

CONTENTS

INTRODUCTION

One would think that the consumption of fish would be equal everywhere. However, some countries in Europe still eat far less than others. This is a pity, because fish is a very healthy food and much easier to digest than meat. The reason for this is that there is no connective tissue in fish: instead, there is protein of high biological value. One needs about 1 gram of protein for every kilogram of bodyweight per day, and thus by eating just a small portion of cod fillet, that need is easily fulfilled. Fish is also very low in calories so is very useful for people on a diet. In addition, there is such a vast array of recipes, that one could serve fish in a different way every day without difficulty.

Never did fish arrive at the fishmonger as fresh as it does today. Modern science makes it possible, even in remote areas, to buy fresh sea fish, river fish still alive, and frozen fish. This is how to treat fish properly and expertly:

Fresh Fish: whole or in fillets: buy in the morning and use the same day. Keep in the refrigerator until needed. You can tell fish is fresh by the red gills, which should be tightly closed, and the bright eyes. And it must smell fresh.

Frozen fish: store in the deep freezer or icemaking compartment of the refrigerator until needed. As a general rule never thaw whole fish or fillets before use.

To clean a whole fish: this is easier than you think; first wash the fish, then make a slit lengthwise on the underside and take out the contents of the belly. Also remove the black membranes, as they make the fish taste bitter.

Most important: rinse the fish inside and out under cold water. Dry carefully with kitchen paper. If necessary, remove any scales with the back of a knife, a fish scaler, or even a cheese grater. Cut the fins on the back and tail with a pair of scissors. Leave about 1 cm/½″ on the body so that the flesh does not get damaged. If you prefer, cut off the head with a sharp knife. If, however, you want to make a fish soup which is going to be strained afterwards, the head should be cooked as well. It makes the soup more flavoursome and aromatic.

Three important steps: rinse—acidulate—salt. These three steps must always be followed, whatever you are going to do with any fish, both whole and in fillets. Whole fish should be rinsed inside and out under cold water after being cleaned and trimmed; fillets do not need cleaning and trimming, but should also be rinsed. Never leave fish hanging around in water; the fish's nutrients might be lost, and certainly the delicate flavour would get lost by leaving it in water longer than necessary. After rinsing, dab the fish dry with kitchen paper.

Then acidulate: that means that the fish should be sprinkled with the juice of a lemon or, if not available, with ½ cup of vinegar and water. This makes the flesh solid and aromatic, and also checks the smell to some extent.

Please note: salt should only be sprinkled on the fish just before you put it in the pan. Never leave it lying around with salt on, as the fish will become soggy and lose flavour.

Cooking: fish can be braised, steamed, poached, fried, baked, grilled, broiled, and deep fried. But one thing you must never do is cook it in boiling water: it then breaks up and loses all flavour and appearance. The idea is to let it cook gently in low heat.

Size of portions: On average, allow 250–375 g/ 8–12 oz/½–¾ lb whole fish and 200 g/6 oz fillet per person.

CARP

The carp forms part of the traditional Christmas and New Year fare in many countries. There are several kinds of carp: some with large scales, some with small scales, and some without scales. Most of them live in ponds. Each carp usually weighs about 1.5–2 kg (3–4 lbs). It is best to buy it ready prepared by the fishmonger, but if you receive it freshly caught, you must take care to remove the black, bitter tasting membranes when you clean the fish.

To scale the fish, use the back of a knife and scrape against the grain. If you want to prepare carp 'blue', do not scale it as you must not damage the skin. It is the delicious covering of mucus on the skin that, in conjunction with vinegar, produces the blue colouring.

Carp Viennese style: this name guarantees a superb fish recipe.

CARP VIENNESE STYLE

Preparation time: 60 mins.
About 605 calories/2532 joules
Accompaniments: peas and boiled potatoes, tossed in
butter and parsley

Metric/Imperial

125g/4 oz streaky bacon
1 carp, about 1.5 kg/3 lbs,
   ready prepared
salt, white pepper
20g/¾ oz butter
1 onion
125ml/4 fl oz white wine
2 tomatoes
50g/2 oz parsley
50g/2 oz dill
1x5ml/1 tsp paprika
1 lemon

American

¼ lb fatty bacon slices
1 carp, about 3 lbs,
   ready prepared
salt, white pepper
1½ tbs butter
1 onion
½ cup white wine
2 tomatoes
4 tbs parsley
4 tbs dill
1 tsp paprika
1 lemon

Slice the bacon and fry in an ovenproof casserole until crisp. Rinse the carp under cold running water inside and out; pat dry with kitchen paper. Rub in salt and pepper. In the casserole, push bacon aside, add butter, and melt. Brown carp on all ides for 10 mins.

Peel onion and chop finely. Add to the casserole and fry with the carp. Add wine. Cover and cook gently for 20 mins. Skin, seed and dice tomatoes. Add to the casserole. Chop parsley and dill finely. Take carp out of the casserole and place on a warmed serving dish. Surround with the bacon slices. Pour juices over and sprinkle with paprika and herbs. Garnish with the lemon, cut into eighths.

BOHEMIAN CARP IN POLISH SAUCE

Preparation time: 55 mins.
About 679 calories/2842 joules
Accompaniments: dumplings and beer

Metric/Imperial

1 carp, about 1 kg/2¼ lbs
juice 1 lemon
For the sauce:
500g/1 lb mixed root
  vegetables
40g/1½ oz margarine
20g/¾ oz flour
575ml/1 pint dark ale
90g/3¼ oz ginger cake
1 bay leaf
4 mustard seeds
1 onion, diced
1 slice lemon
1x15ml/1 tbs seedless
 raisins
1x15ml/1 tbs flaked
almonds
juice ½ lemon
salt, sugar

American

1 carp, about 2¼ lbs
juice 1 lemon

1 lb mixed root
  vegetables
3 tbs margarine
1½ tbs flour
2½ cups dark beer
¼ lb ginger cake
1 bay leaf
4 mustard seeds
1 onion, diced
1 slice lemon
1 tbs seedless
  raisins

1 tbs flaked almonds
juice ½ lemon
salt, sugar

Scale, gut, and wash the carp. Cut into portions. Sprinkle with lemon juice.
For the sauce:
Wash, trim, and roughly chop vegetables. Soften in hot margarine. Sprinkle with flour and brown. Add ½ of the beer and pour the other ½ over the ginger cake. Add the bay leaf, mustard seeds, diced onion, and slice of lemon to the sauce. When the ginger cake has been well soaked, add to the sauce. Cook gently for 20 mins. Add the slices of carp, and simmer very gently for 25 mins. until cooked. Add the raisins and almonds, and season with salt, sugar, and lemon juice.

Bohemian carp in Polish sauce.

CARP SLICES PROVENÇAL

Preparation time: 45 mins.
About 435 calories/1821 joules

Metric/Imperial	American
4 fillets of carp, each 200g/7 oz	4 fillets of carp, each 7 oz
2x15ml/2 tbs oil	2 tbs oil
3 onions, diced	3 onions, diced
25g/1 oz margarine	2 tbs margarine
4 tomatoes	4 tomatoes
1 clove garlic	1 clove garlic
salt	salt
125ml/4 fl oz white wine	½ cup white wine
2x15ml/2 tbs dried breadcrumbs	2 tbs dried breadcrumbs
20g/¾ oz butter	1½ tbs butter
50g/2 oz parsley	4 tbs parsley
1 sprig tarragon	1 sprig tarragon
10 black olives	10 black olives
2 hardboiled eggs	2 hardboiled eggs

Preheat oven to 200°C/400°F/Gas 6. Rinse the fillets of carp under cold water and pat dry. Heat oil in a frying pan. Fry fillets for 3 mins. on each side until browned. Keep warm. Heat margarine in a saucepan, and fry onions for 5 mins. until browned. Skin, seed, and dice tomatoes. Peel clove of garlic and crush with a little salt. Mix with the onions. Put half the onion mixture in an ovenproof dish. Cover with half the tomatoes. Season the fillets of carp with salt and place on top. Pour over the juices and cover with the remaining onions and tomatoes. Pour over the wine and sprinkle with the breadcrumbs. Dot with butter. Place in the preheated oven on the middle shelf for 15 mins.
Chop parsley and tarragon finely. Halve the olives and remove stones. Remove the fish from the oven and sprinkle with the herbs and olives. Garnish with the eggs, cut into quarters.

'BLUE' CARP

Preparation time: 45 mins.
About 455 calories/1904 joules
Accompaniments: creamed horseradish and
boiled potatoes

Metric/Imperial	American
1 carp, about 1.5kg/3 lbs	1 carp, about 3 lbs
salt	salt
125ml/4 fl oz vinegar	½ cup vinegar
125ml/4 fl oz white wine	½ cup white wine
375ml/12 fl oz water	1½ cups water
1 onion	1 onion
1 bay leaf	1 bay leaf
4 peppercorns	4 peppercorns
½ lemon	½ lemon
40g/1½ oz butter	3 tbs butter
For the garnish:	
8 lettuce leaves	8 lettuce leaves
1 tomato, sliced	1 tomato, sliced
½ lemon	½ lemon
1x15ml/1 tbs creamed	1 tbs creamed
horseradish	horseradish

Cut open the belly of the carp with a sharp knife, and gut. Wash carefully so as not to damage the delicate covering mucus on the skin. Pat dry the inside and season with salt. Do not scale. Place the fish in a basin. Heat the vinegar to boiling point and pour over the fish. Leave for 10 mins. in an airy place. Then lift on to a serving plate, reserving the vinegar.

Heat the wine, water, and vinegar in a large casserole. Peel the onion and cut in two. Add to the liquid, together with the bay leaf, peppercorns, and lemon. Place the carp in the casserole and cook on the lowest possible heat for 20 mins. Carefully lift the carp out with two draining spoons, drain, and arrange on a preheated serving dish. Garnish with the lettuce, sliced tomato, and ½ lemon filled with the creamed horseradish. Melt the butter and serve separately.

'Blue' Carp.

COD

Today, more cod is caught than any other sea fish, apart from the herring, in the whole of northern Europe. Cod is usually available as fresh fish: the main fishing areas are near the banks of Newfoundland, Iceland, the Lofoten Islands, and the Barents Sea. The cod is not only one of the most prolific but also one of the most voracious fish of prey. In its lifetime, which may be 20 years, it can reach a length of up to 150cm/5 ft and a weight of up to 50kg/110lbs. It is usually caught, however, when it is younger and less heavy: in the Atlantic Ocean at 10–20kg/22–44lbs, in the North Sea at about 5–7kg/11–15lbs. The Baltic fishermen also often find codling in their nets.

FRIED COD

Preparation time: 50 mins.
About 750 calories/3140 joules
Accompaniments: potato salad or boiled potatoes and
green salad

Metric/Imperial

1kg/2¼ lbs cod, gutted
lemon juice
salt
50g/2 oz streaky bacon
6x15ml/6 tbs oil
1 large onion
2 eggs
4x15ml/4 tbs water
100g/4 oz dried
   breadcrumbs
fat for frying
30g/1 oz butter
1x15ml/1 tbs flour
250ml/8 fl oz water
seasoning
For the garnish:
few lettuce leaves
lemon wedges
parsley

American

2¼ lbs cod, gutted
lemon juice
salt
2 fatty bacon slices
6 tbs oil
1 large onion
2 eggs
4 tbs water
1 cup dried
   breadcrumbs
fat for frying
2 tbs butter
1 tbs flour
1 cup water
seasoning

few lettuce leaves
lemon wedges
parsley

Rinse fish under cold water and cut in two. Remove the bones. Sprinkle with lemon juice and salt. Dice the bacon and fry gently until the fat runs. Add 3x15ml/3 tbs oil. Peel the onion and fry whole. Beat the eggs with water. Dip each half of fish first in the egg and then in the breadcrumbs to coat completely. Fry in the fat and remaining oil until golden brown. Remove the fish, bacon, and onion and keep warm. Add the butter to the pan, sprinkle with flour, brown, and mix in the water. Cook the sauce for 10 mins. Season. Arrange the fish on the lettuce leaves. Garnish with the bacon, onion, lemon wedges, and parsley.

Fried cod garnished with diced bacon, onion and lemon wedges.

Cod cutlets gourmet style.

COD CUTLETS GOURMET STYLE

Preparation time: 1 hr. 15 mins.
About 390 calories/1633 joules

Metric/Imperial	American
4 cod cutlets, each 200g/7 oz	4 cod cutlets, each 7 oz
juice 1 lemon	juice 1 lemon
salt, white pepper	salt, white pepper
40g/1½ oz butter	3 tbs butter
1 onion, sliced	1 onion, sliced
few sprigs parsley	few sprigs parsley
1 glass dry white wine	1 glass dry white wine
For the sauce:	
40g/1½ oz butter	3 tbs butter
25g/1oz flour	2 tbs flour
250ml/8 fl oz hot chicken stock	1 cup hot chicken stock
1 glass white wine	1 glass white wine
150g/5 oz button mushrooms	5 oz mushrooms
100g/4 oz frozen prawns	¼ lb shrimps
2x5ml/2 tsp lemon juice	2 tsp lemon juice
2 egg yolks	2 egg yolks
1 lemon for garnish	1 lemon for garnish

Wash cutlets and pat dry. Sprinkle with lemon juice and leave for 10 mins. Season with salt and pepper. Melt the butter in a large frying pan. Brown the cutlets for 10 mins. each side. Add the sliced onion and brown. Chop half the parsley and add to the pan. (Keep the remainder for garnish.) Pour in wine and cook for a further 5 mins. Arrange cutlets on a serving plate and keep warm. Reserve the cooking liquor.

For the sauce, melt the butter in a saucepan, and stir in the flour. Add the fish liquor and the hot stock and stir vigorously. Add the white wine and simmer gently. Slice the mushrooms thinly (reserving a few for the garnish) and add to the sauce, together with the thawed prawns. Cook gently for 15 mins. Seasons with lemon juice and salt. Take a little sauce and mix with the beaten egg yolks. Pour back into the sauce but do not let it boil as it will then curdle. Cover the cutlets with the sauce. Garnish with the remaining parsley, sliced mushrooms, and the lemon cut in wedges.

MEXICAN BRAISED COD

Preparation time: 40 mins.
About 315 calories/1318 joules
Accompaniments: rice and a salad of green and
red peppers. Drink beer or Spanish red wine with it.

Metric/Imperial

2 onions
4x15ml/4 tbs oil
4 fillets of cod
    each 250g/8 oz
pinch of garlic salt, salt
2½ml/½ tsp cayenne
    pepper
1 small jar red pimento
    peppers
few sprigs parsley

American

2 onions
4 tbs oil
4 fillets of cod
    each ½ lb
pinch of garlic salt, salt
½ tsp cayenne pepper

1 small jar red
    peppers
few sprigs parsley

Preheat oven to 220°C/425°F/Gas 7. Cut the onions into rings. Heat the oil in an ovenproof casserole and fry the onions for about 5 mins. until soft. Wash the fillets of cod and pat dry. Rub in a mixture of salt, garlic salt, and cayenne pepper. Lay on top of the onions.

Drain the peppers and cut into 1cm/½ in. strips. Lay these decoratively over the fish. Place the casserole in the preheated oven on the bottom shelf for 20 mins. Chop the parsley finely, and sprinkle over the dish before serving.

COD ROLLS WITH MUSHROOM STUFFING

Preparation time: 55 mins.
About 410 calories/1715 joules

Metric/Imperial

1kg/2¼ lbs fillets of cod
juice of 1 lemon
250g/8 oz button
    mushrooms
1 small onion
25g/1 oz butter or
    margarine
2x15ml/2 tbs dried
    breadcrumbs
2 eggs
salt
margarine for greasing
250ml/8 fl oz soured
    cream
white pepper

American

2¼ lbs fillets of cod
juice of 1 lemon
½ lb mushrooms

1 small onion
2 tbs butter or
    margarine
2 tbs dried
    breadcrumbs
2 eggs
salt
margarine for greasing
1 cup sour cream

white pepper

Wash the fillets, pat dry, and cut into four pieces. Sprinkle with lemon juice. Dice the onion. Melt butter or margarine and soften the onion and mushrooms. Add the breadcrumbs and one egg. Mix well. Spread most of the stuffing on the salted cod fillets. Roll up and fasten with cocktail sticks. Grease an ovenproof dish and carefully place the fish rolls upright in it. Surround with remaining stuffing.

Stir the other egg and the soured cream together, season with salt and pepper, and pour over the fish. Place in the preheated oven for 30 mins.

Cod rolls with mushroom stuffing.

Cod Malmö is a typical Scandinavian fish dish.

COD MALMÖ

Preparation time: 60 mins.
About 525 calories/2200 joules
Accompaniments: peas and boiled potatoes, tossed in butter and parsley

Metric/Imperial

1kg/2¼ lbs fillets of cod
lemon juice
250g/8 oz frozen peas
3 carrots
175g/6 oz button
  mushrooms
375g/12 oz tinned
  asparagus pieces
margarine for greasing
few sprigs parsley
2 egg yolks
250ml/8 fl oz single cream
white pepper, salt
3x15ml/3 tbs dried
  breadcrumbs
3x15ml/3 tbs Emmenthal
  cheese, grated
25g/1 oz butter

American

2¼ lbs fillets of cod
lemon juice
½ lb frozen peas
3 carrots
6 oz mushrooms

12 oz canned
  asparagus pieces
margarine for greasing
few sprigs parsley
2 egg yolks
1 cup light cream
white pepper, salt
3 tbs dried
  breadcrumbs
3 tbs Swiss cheese,
  grated
2 tbs butter

Preheat oven to 220°C/425°F/Gas 7. Wash the cod fillets and cut into largish cubes. Sprinkle with lemon juice. Slice the carrots very thinly. Drain the asparagus. Grease an ovenproof deep dish with margarine. Place one layer of fish in the bottom and then alternate layers of vegetables and fish. Chop the parsley and sprinkle over the dish.

Mix the egg yolks, cream, salt, and pepper and pour over the fish mixture. Cover with breadcrumbs, then cheese, and dot with butter. Place in the preheated oven for 40 mins.

INDIAN FISH KEBABS

Preparation time: 1 hr. 10 mins.
About 585 calories/2448 joules
Accompaniments: mixed salad and boiled rice

Metric/Imperial

500g/1 lb fillet of cod
juice ½ lemon
salt
2 apples
2 bananas
2x5ml/2 tsp curry powder
½ red and ½ green
  pepper
150g/5 oz streaky bacon
margarine for greasing
125ml/4 fl oz white wine
few sprigs parsley
For the sauce:
3x15ml/3 tbs tomato
  ketchup mixed with
  1x5ml/1 tsp curry
  powder
125ml/4 fl oz soured
  cream
25g/1 oz Parmesan cheese
  grated
pinch of sugar
salt, pepper

American

1 lb fillet of cod
juice ½ lemon
salt
2 apples
2 bananas
2 tsp curry powder
½ red and ½ green
  pepper
5 oz fatty bacon slices
margarine for greasing
½ cup white wine
few sprigs parsley

3 tbs tomato ketchup
  mixed with 1 tsp
  curry powder

½ cup sour cream

2 tbs Parmesan cheese,
  grated
pinch of sugar
salt, pepper

Preheat oven to 200°C/400°F/Gas 6. Rinse the fillet of cod, pat dry, sprinkle with lemon juice and leave for 10 mins. Season with salt and cut into even cubes. Cut the apples in cubes and the peeled bananas in thick slices. Roll in curry powder. Seed the peppers, and cut in cubes. Pour boiling water over them and leave for 5 mins. Then drain. Cut the bacon in thick pieces and fry lightly until the fat runs. Reserve the fat.

Thread all the ingredients alternately on to 8 wooden skewers. Well grease an ovenproof shallow dish with margarine, insert the fish skewers, and pour over the bacon fat and white wine. Place in preheated oven on the centre shelf for 20 mins.

Arrange the fish kebabs on a heated serving plate and garnish with parsley. Pour the cooking juices into a small saucepan, scraping all the bits off the bottom. Stir in the curry flavoured tomato ketchup, soured cream, and Parmesan cheese. Mix well and heat until boiling point. Remove from the heat and season well with salt, pepper, and sugar. Pour over the fish kebabs or serve separately.

Indian fish kebabs.

Flemish cod.

Cod au gratin.

FLEMISH COD

Preparation time: 45 mins.
About 370 calories/1549 joules

Metric/Imperial	American
4 fillets of cod, each 200g/6 oz	4 fillets of cod, each 6 oz
20g/¾ oz butter	1½ tbs butter
2 lemons	2 lemons
3 onions, chopped	3 onions, chopped
few sprigs parsley	few sprigs parsley
few sprigs dill	few sprigs dill
salt, white pepper	salt, white pepper
fish seasoning	fish seasoning
125ml/4 fl oz white wine	½ cup white wine
6x15ml/6 tbs dried breadcrumbs	6 tbs dried breadcrumbs
40g/1½ oz butter	3 tbs butter

Preheat oven to 220°C/425°F/Gas 7. Wash the fillets of cod and pat dry. Cut in 5cm/2 in. pieces. Grease an ovenproof dish with butter and place the fish pieces in it. Slice the lemons thinly and cover the fillets with them. Sprinkle the chopped onions on top. Chop the parsley and dill finely and scatter over the fish, together with salt, pepper, and fish seasoning. Pour wine over. Cover with breadcrumbs, and dot with butter. Place in the preheated oven on the bottom shelf for 25 mins.

COD AU GRATIN

Preparation time: 55 mins.
About 655 calories/2741 joules
Accompaniment: cucumber salad with dill and cream dressing

Metric/Imperial	American
500g/1 lb potatoes	1 lb potatoes
1 kg/2 lbs cod	2 lbs cod
500ml/16 fl oz water	2 cups water
salt	salt
2x15ml/2 tbs wine vinegar	2 tbs wine vinegar
1 bay leaf	1 bay leaf
4 peppercorns	4 peppercorns
For the Béchamel sauce:	
40g/1½ oz butter	3 tbs butter
1 onion, diced	1 onion, diced
40g/1½ oz ham, diced	1 slice ham, diced
40g/1½ oz flour	3 tbs flour
250ml/8 fl oz stock	1 cup stock
250ml/8 fl oz milk	1 cup milk
salt, white pepper	salt, white pepper
In addition:	
125ml/4 fl oz milk	½ cup milk
1 egg yolk	1 egg yolk
pinch of grated nutmeg	pinch of grated nutmeg
butter for greasing	butter for greasing
50g/2 oz Emmenthal cheese, grated	1 cup Swiss cheese, grated
25g/1 oz butter	2 tbs butter
2 tomatoes	2 tomatoes

Preheat oven to 230°C/450°F/Gas 8. Boil potatoes in salted water until cooked. Wash the fish and pat dry. Add salt, vinegar, bay leaf, and peppercorns to the water, and bring to boil in a large saucepan. Add the fish and simmer gently for 7 mins. For the sauce, melt the butter in a saucepan and fry the diced onion and ham until lightly coloured. Add the flour and cook for 3 mins., stirring constantly. Pour in the stock and milk and cook for 10 mins., stirring continuously. Season with salt and pepper. Drain and mash the potatoes. Heat the milk and pour over them. Stir with a wire whisk. Then stir in the egg yolk. Season with nutmeg and salt.
Grease an ovenproof casserole and line with potato purée. Cover with 8x15ml/8 tbs of the sauce. Drain the fish, flake, and remove the bones. Place in the casserole. Pour over the remaining sauce. Sprinkle with cheese and dot with butter. Place in the preheated oven on the bottom shelf for 15 mins. Garnish with tomatoes, skinned and quartered.

COD IN HERB AND PRAWN SAUCE

Preparation time: 50 mins.
About 425 calories/1779 joules
Accompaniments: grilled tomatoes and boiled potatoes,
tossed in butter and parsley

Metric/Imperial	American
4 fillets of cod, each 250g/8 oz	4 fillets of cod, each ½ lb
salt	salt
juice 1 lemon	juice 1 lemon
3x15ml/3 tbs hot water	3 tbs hot water
For the sauce:	
50g/2 oz parsley	4 tbs parsley
50g/2 oz fresh, or 1x15ml/1 tbs dried dill	4 tbs fresh or or 1 tbs dried dill
30g/1 oz fresh or 1x15ml/1 tsp dried chervil	2 tbs fresh or 1 tsp dried chervil
30g/1 oz butter	2 tbs butter
30g/1 oz flour	2 tbs flour
250ml/8 fl oz fish liquor	1 cup fish liquor
125ml/4 fl oz cream	½ cup cream
pepper	pepper
170g/6 oz prawns	6 oz shrimps
1 small pickled gherkin	1 small pickled gherkin

Preheat oven to 220°C/425°F/Gas 7. Rinse the cod fillet under cold water and pat dry. Salt slightly and sprinkle with lemon juice. Place in an ovenproof dish. Pour over 3x15ml/3 tbs hot water. Place in the preheated oven on the bottom shelf for 25 mins.
In the meantime, chop the parsley, dill, and chervil finely. When cooked, drain the fish and keep warm, reserving the cooking liquor. Melt the butter in a pan and add the flour. Cook for 3 mins., stirring constantly. Make the fish liquor up to 250ml/8 fl oz/1 cup with water. Add gradually to the roux and cook for 5 mins. Remove from the heat and stir in the cream. Season with pepper. Add prawns and chopped herbs. Heat but do not allow to boil. Pour the sauce over the fish and garnish with the sliced gherkin.

MALAYSIAN GINGER FISH

Preparation time: 30 mins.
About 355 calories/1486 joules
Accompaniments: saffron rice

Metric/Imperial	American
4 fillets of cod, each 250g/8 oz	4 fillets of cod, each ½ lb
juice 1 lemon	juice 1 lemon
salt	salt
2x15ml/2 tbs flour	2 tbs flour
4x15ml/4 tbs olive oil	4 tbs olive oil
garlic salt	garlic salt
25g/1 oz preserved stem ginger	1 oz preserved stem ginger
250ml/8 fl oz hot stock	1 cup hot stock
2x15ml/2 tbs white wine vinegar	2 tbs white wine vinegar
1 large pinch allspice	1 large pinch allspice
2x15ml/2 tsp cornflour	2 tsp cornstarch
2x15ml/2 tbs soya sauce	2 tbs soya sauce
4x15ml/4 tbs cream	4 tbs cream

Malaysia's fishermen naturally catch a lot of fish that are totally unknown to us. This savoury way of cooking fish, however, is equally suitable for more familiar fish like the cod.
Rinse the fillets, and pat dry. Sprinkle with lemon juice and salt. Roll in flour. Heat the olive oil in a frying pan and fry the fish for 6 mins. each side until golden. Season with garlic salt.
Meanwhile, dice the stem ginger. Remove the fish from the frying pan and keep warm on a heated serving plate. Add the ginger to the fat remaining in the pan and pour in the stock and vinegar. Sprinkle in the allspice. Mix the cornflour with a little water and add to thicken the sauce. Bring to the boil. Add the soya sauce. Remove from the heat and stir in the cream. Pour some of the sauce over the fillets of cod, and serve the rest separately.

Cod in herb and prawn sauce.

Malaysian fish curry.

MALAYSIAN FISH CURRY

Preparation time: 35 mins.
About 505 calories/2114 joules
Accompaniments: green salad and boiled rice

Metric/Imperial	American
800g/1¾ lbs cod fillets	**1¾ lbs cod fillets**
2x15ml/2 tbs lemon juice	**2 tbs lemon juice**
salt	**salt**
2x15ml/2 tbs curry powder	**2 tbs curry powder**
3x15ml/3 tbs flour	**3 tbs flour**
4x15ml/4 tbs peanut oil	**4 tbs peanut oil**
3 onions	**3 onions**
10g/½ oz butter or margarine	**1 tbs butter or margarine**
4x15ml/4 tbs milk	**4 tbs milk**
1x15ml/1 tbs flour	**1 tbs flour**
50g/2 oz salted peanuts	**⅓ cup salted peanuts**
2½ml/½ tsp powdered ginger	**½ tsp powdered ginger**
125ml/4 fl oz	**½ cup cream**

Wash the fish and pat dry. Cut into 5cm/2 in. cubes, sprinkle with lemon juice, cover, and leave for 10 mins. Season with salt and 1x15ml/1 tbs of curry powder. Roll in the flour. Heat the peanut oil in a large frying pan. Fry the fish until golden brown. Take out, place on a serving dish and keep warm. Slice the onions thinly. Heat the butter or margarine in a second frying pan. Dip the onion rings first in the milk and then in the flour. Fry for 5 mins. until golden. Keep warm. Add the peanuts, ginger, cream, and remaining curry powder to the frying pan in which you fried the fish. Cook gently for 2 mins. Pour over the fish and garnish with the fried onion rings.

MERLUZA A LA VASCA
Cod Basque style

Preparation time: 55 mins.
About 415 calories/1737 joules
Accompaniments: salad of red and green peppers with oil
and vinegar dressing, and boiled rice. Drink a Spanish or
Italian red wine with it.

Metric/Imperial	American
800g/1¾ lbs cod fillets	1¾ lb cod fillets
salt	salt
juice 1 lemon	juice 1 lemon
For the paprika purée:	
2 onions	2 onions
3 cloves garlic	3 cloves garlic
salt	salt
4 red peppers	4 red peppers
4x15ml/4 tbs olive oil	4 tbs olive oil
1 bay leaf	1 bay leaf
5 peppercorns, crushed	5 peppercorns, crushed
4 cloves	4 cloves
1x15ml/1 tbs olive oil	1 tbs olive oil
for greasing	for greasing
For the garnish:	
few sprigs parsley	few sprigs parsley
220g/7 oz tinned asparagus	7 oz canned asparagus
4 hardboiled eggs	4 hardboiled eggs

Preheat oven to 220°C/425°F/Gas 7. Wash and pat dry the fish and divide into eight pieces. Sprinkle with salt and lemon juice.

For the paprika purée, chop the onions finely and crush the garlic with a little salt. Dice the red peppers. Heat the oil in a frying pan. Soften the onions and garlic gently for 5 mins. Add the peppers, bay leaf, crushed peppercorns, and cloves. Cover and cook gently for 15 mins. Pass through a strainer or remove the spices and mix to a purée in an electric mixer.

Grease an ovenproof dish with olive oil. Place the cod on it and spread the paprika purée over it. Bake in the preheated oven on the middle shelf for 20 mins.

In the meantime, for the garnish, chop the parsley, and heat the asparagus in its liquid in a saucepan. Cut the eggs into wedges.

Take the cod out of the oven and arrange on a preheated serving dish. Surround with the egg wedges and 2 or 3 asparagus spears alternately. Sprinkle with chopped parsley and serve.

TIP
If you want to purée the peppers in an electric mixer for the Merluza a la Vasca (cod Basque style), cool them for 10–15 mins. first.

A Spanish dish, Merluza à la Vasca.

COLEY

Coley is a member of the cod family. It can reach a length of up to 120cm/4 ft and weigh up to 10kg/22 lbs. It has a bluish-black back, and a greyish-white belly, and a black mouth. The flesh is silvery grey. It tastes very much like cod.

The coley's habitat is in the Atlantic Ocean, from the Bay of Biscay up to Greenland. The main catch areas, however, are the waters south of Iceland and west of the Norwegian coasts up to Spitzbergen. Fresh coley is usually available as fillets or cutlets.

Coley, Nice style.

COLEY, NICE STYLE

Preparation time: 35 mins.
About 430 calories/1799 joules

Metric/Imperial

4 coley cutlets weighing
   200g/6 oz each
juice 1 lemon
salt, white pepper
4x15ml/4 tbs olive oil
4x15ml/4 tbs flour
For the garnish:
250g/8 oz tomatoes
250g/8 oz green beans,
   cooked and drained
25g/1 oz butter
few lettuce leaves
2 hardboiled eggs
few sprigs parsley
12 anchovy fillets
12 stuffed green olives

American

4 coley cutlets
   weighing 6 oz each
juice 1 lemon
salt, white pepper
4 tbs olive oil
4 tbs flour

½ lb tomatoes
½ lb green beans,
   cooked and drained
2 tbs butter
few lettuce leaves
2 hardboiled eggs
few sprigs parsley
12 anchovy fillets
12 stuffed green olives

Rinse the coley cutlets briefly under cold water and pat dry. Sprinkle with lemon juice and leave to marinade for 10 mins. Season with salt and pepper and brush all over with olive oil. Sprinkle with flour. Line a grill pan with aluminium foil, place the grill rack in position and grill the cutlets under a hot grill for 8 mins. Turn after 4 mins. Meanwhile slice the tomatoes. Melt the butter and reheat the drained beans. Season with salt and pepper.

Peel the eggs and cut into wedges. Finely chop the parsley. Drain the anchovy fillets and olives. Slice the olives.

Line a serving platter with the lettuce leaves and arrange the drained coley cutlets on top. Surround with the sliced tomatoes, beans and egg wedges. Arrange the anchovy fillets in a criss cross pattern over the fish and sprinkle the dish with the sliced olives and chopped parsley. Serve immediately.

COLEY WITH HERBS

Preparation time: 45 mins.
About 345 calories/1444 joules
Accompaniments: green salad and boiled potatoes or rice

Metric/Imperial

4 fillets of coley,
    each 150g/5 oz
juice 1 lemon
salt
100g/4 oz streaky bacon
2 onions
500g/1 lb tomatoes
few sprigs each chives,
    dill, and parsley
½ carton mustard and
    cress
2½ml/½ tsp each dried
    chervil and tarragon
125ml/4 fl oz soured cream
white pepper
2x15ml/2 tbs dried
    breadcrumbs

American

4 fillets of coley,
    each 5 oz
juice 1 lemon
salt
¼ lb fatty bacon slices
2 onions
1 lb tomatoes
few sprigs each chives,
    dill, and parsley
½ carton of cress

½ tsp each dried
    chervil and tarragon
½ cup sour cream
white pepper
2 tbs dried
    breadcrumbs

Preheat oven to 180°C/350°F/Gas 4. Rinse the coley fillets under cold water and pat dry. Sprinkle with lemon juice and salt and set aside.

Dice the bacon and fry gently until the fat runs. Add the chopped onion and cook for 5 mins. until transparent. Skin the tomatoes, remove the core and cut in slices. Finely chop the fresh herbs and mix with the soured cream. Season with salt and pepper.

Spread half of the bacon and onion mixture over the bottom of an ovenproof dish, cover with the sliced tomatoes and top with the fish fillets. Pour over the herb and cream mixture, top with the remaining bacon and onion mixture and sprinkle with breadcrumbs. Cover and place in the preheated oven on the centre shelf for 15 mins.

Serve the fish in the ovenproof dish.

Coley with herbs.

Zarzuela.

ZARZUELA

Preparation time: 50 mins.
About 410 calories/1716 joules

Metric/Imperial

350g/11 oz frozen squid
12 frozen scampi
375g/12 oz fresh mussels
375g/12 oz coley or cod
2 onions
4x15ml/4 tbs olive oil
5 sprigs parsley
4 cloves garlic
4 tomatoes
salt, white pepper
250ml/8 fl oz white wine
1x15ml/1 tbs brandy
juice ½ lemon

American

11 oz frozen squid
12 frozen scampi
¾ lb fresh mussels
¾ lb coley or cod
2 onions
4 tbs olive oil
5 sprigs parsley
4 cloves garlic
4 tomatoes
salt, white pepper
1 cup white wine
1 tbs brandy
juice ½ lemon

Zarzuela is the Spanish name for a musical comedy. Maybe this fish dish is called that because all the ingredients mix together in perfect harmony.

Defrost the squid and scampi according to instructions on the packet. Scrub the mussels well under cold running water and drain. Carefully cut off the beards. Rinse the coley or cod, pat dry, and cut in bite-sized pieces. Dice the onions finely.

Heat the oil in a frying pan and fry the onions for 5 mins. until golden. Slice the squid and add to the pan with the scampi, mussels, and coley or cod. Fry, turning frequently, until the mussels have opened their shells, about 8 mins. In the meantime, finely chop the parsley and garlic, and skin and dice the tomatoes. Add them all to the pan and season well. Pour in the white wine and brandy. Simmer for 15 mins. The liquid should thicken slightly. Remove the frying pan from the heat, sprinkle with lemon juice, and serve the zarzuela straight from the pan.

Note:
If you like olives, a few could be sliced and added to the dish at the end of the cooking time.

CASSEROLE FISH

Preparation time: 1 hr. 20 mins.
About 205 calories/858 joules

Metric/Imperial

1 kg/2¼ lbs fillets of
  cod or haddock
500g/1 lb potatoes
250g/½ lb carrots
2 celery sticks
2 leeks
2 onions
100g/4oz streaky bacon
salt, white pepper
grated nutmeg
250ml/8 fl oz hot stock
parsley for garnish

American

2¼ lbs fillets of
  cod or haddock
1 lb potatoes
½ lb carrots
2 celery sticks
2 leeks
2 onions
¼ lb fatty bacon slices
salt, white pepper
grated nutmeg
1 cup hot stock
parsley for garnish

Rinse the fillets, pat dry, and cut in 2½cm/1 in. cubes. Dice the potatoes, carrots, and celery the same size as the fish.

Cut the leeks and onions in thick slices. Chop the bacon and gently fry in an ovenproof casserole until the fat runs. Layer the fish and vegetables in the dish, and season with salt, pepper, and nutmeg. Pour over the stock, cover, and poach gently for 50 mins. Garnish with finely chopped parsley.

'BLUE' EEL

Preparation time: 55 mins.
About 748 calories/3281 joules
Accompaniments: boiled potatoes tossed in butter and parsley, and a delicate white wine

Metric/Imperial	American
1 eel, about 1kg/2¼ lbs	1 eel, about 2¼ lbs
salt	salt
250ml/8 fl oz hot vinegar	1 cup hot vinegar

For the liquor:	
2 litres/3½ pints water	9 cups water
25g/1 oz salt	2 tbs salt
1 onion	1 onion
1 dash white wine	1 dash white wine
1 bay leaf	1 bay leaf
6 peppercorns	6 peppercorns
piece of lemon	piece of lemon
1 carrot	1 carrot
1 parsley stalk	1 parsley stalk
a little thyme	a little thyme

For the Hollandaise sauce:	
2 egg yolks	2 egg yolks
1 dash white wine	1 dash white wine
125g/4½ oz butter	¾ cup butter
1 dash Worcester sauce	1 dash Worcester sauce
lemon juice, salt, pepper	lemon juice, salt, pepper

For the garnish:	
3 lemons	3 lemons
few sprigs dill	few sprigs dill
2x5ml/2 tsp capers	2 tsp capers
a little parsley	a little parsley

Gut the eel, but do not skin. Season the inside. Tie head and tail together (this is called 'trussing'). Pour the hot vinegar over the fish. This produces the 'blue' colour. Heat the water and bring to the boil with the ingredients for the liquor. Add the eel and poach gently for 20–30 mins. Do not allow to boil or the fish might break up.

In the meantime, prepare the Hollandaise sauce. Whisk the egg yolks with the wine over a pan of warm water until light and frothy. Melt the butter, and add to the egg yolks gradually while lukewarm. Season with Worcester sauce, lemon juice, salt, and pepper. Remove the eel from the liquor and arrange it on a serving dish in one piece. Garnish with 4 halves of lemon and sprigs of dill. Cut remaining lemon in half and remove flesh. Fill the empty lemon shells with the Hollandaise sauce, and garnish with capers and chopped parsley. Alternatively, pour the sauce into a small serving bowl and place in the centre of the eel 'ring'.

EEL PROVENÇAL

Preparation time: 65 mins.
About 767 calories/3210 joules
Accompaniments: mixed salad and new potatoes

Metric/Imperial	American
1 eel, about 1kg/2¼ lbs	1 eel, about 2¼ lbs
lemon juice	lemon juice
salt, white pepper	salt, white pepper
5x15ml/5 tbs olive oil	5 tbs olive oil
2 onions, diced	2 onions, diced
1 clove garlic, crushed	1 clove garlic, crushed
250ml/8 fl oz dry white wine	1 cup dry white wine
1x15ml/1 tbs anchovy paste	1 tbs anchovy paste
500g/1 lb ripe tomatoes	1 lb ripe tomatoes
few sprigs parsley	few sprigs parsley

Clean the eel. Cut in 5cm/2 in. pieces. Sprinkle with lemon juice, salt, and pepper. Heat the oil in a casserole, and soften the diced onions and crushed garlic. Fry the pieces of eel until golden. Add the wine. Season with anchovy paste. Skin the tomatoes and cut in half. Add to the fish. Cook gently for 20 mins. Season with salt and pepper. Sprinkle with chopped parsley.

'Blue' Eel with Hollandaise sauce.

BAKED EEL

Preparation time: 55 mins.
555 calories/2323 joules
Accompaniments: dry toast, or boiled potatoes tossed in butter and parsley, and cucumber salad

Only fresh eel is suitable for baking in the oven.

Metric/Imperial	American
1 eel, about 1 kg/2¼ lbs	1 eel, about 2¼ lbs
salt	salt
1 lemon	1 lemon
1 bay leaf	1 bay leaf
50g/2 oz butter	2 tbs butter

Gut and wash the eel. Cut in 8cm/4 in. pieces and sprinkle with salt. Place in a single layer in an ovenproof dish. Tuck a slice of lemon with the pips removed and a piece of bay leaf between each portion of eel. Dot with butter. Bake in a hot oven for about 30 mins. until nicely browned.

TIP
It is not difficult to skin an eel. First cut off the fins and make a cut across behind the head. The skin is pulled off like a glove in one piece. Hang the fish on a hook to make the job easier.

TIP
Eels are very slippery. To make them easier to skin, rub with coarse salt.

ITALIAN EEL

Preparation time: 60 mins.
About 905 calories/3788 joules
Accompaniments: buttered toast and an Italian red wine

Metric/Imperial	American
1 eel, about 1kg/2¼ lbs	1 eel, about 2¼ lbs
For the marinade:	
125ml/4 fl oz olive oil	½ cup olive oil
juice 1 lemon	juice 1 lemon
pinch of dried oregano	pinch of dried oregano
4x15ml/4 tbs oil for frying	4 tbs oil for frying
salt, white pepper	salt, white pepper

Gut, skin and wash the eel. Pat dry and cut into 2½cm/1 in. slices.
For the marinade, mix the olive oil with the lemon juice and oregano in a bowl. Add the eel and leave for 20 mins. Take out and pat dry.
Heat the oil in a frying pan until smoking hot and fry the eel pieces for 10 mins. on all sides. Reduce the temperature and continue cooking for another 20 mins. Arrange on a preheated serving dish. Season the marinade well with salt and pepper. Pour over the fish and serve immediately.

EEL ROLLS

Preparation time: 2 hrs. 10 mins.
777 calories/3252 joules
Accompaniments: buttered toast or sautéed potatoes

Metric/Imperial	American
2 eels, each 500g/1 lb	2 eels, each 1 lb
salt, pepper	salt, pepper
For the stuffing:	
250g/8 oz fillet of coley	½ lb fillet of coley
½ onion	½ onion
1 stale bread roll	1 stale bread roll
25g/1 oz butter	2 tbs butter
1 egg	1 egg
salt, pepper, nutmeg	salt, pepper, nutmeg
3–4x15ml/3–4 tbs soured cream	3–4 tbs sour cream
50g/2 oz cooked tongue	2 slices cooked tongue
2 small pickled gherkins	2 small gherkins
For the liquor:	
1½ litres/2½ pints water	6¼ cups water
1 onion, sliced	1 onion, sliced
500g/1 lb mixed root vegetables	1 lb mixed root vegetables
a few peppercorns	a few peppercorns
1 bay leaf	1 bay leaf
larch pinch of salt	large pinch of salt
125ml/4 fl oz white wine	½ cup white wine
2x15ml/2 tbs gelatine	2 tbs gelatine
mayonnaise	mayonnaise
few sprigs parsley	few sprigs parsley

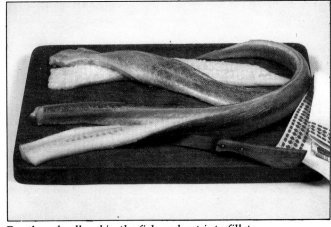

For the eel rolls, skin the fish and cut into fillets.

Have all the ingredients for the stuffing ready chopped.

Wash the eels, cut off the fins, skin, and gut. Cut off the head. Carefully remove the bones. Keep the skin, head, and bones but discard the stomach contents. This should make four fillets. Rinse them, pat dry and flatten slightly. Sprinkle with salt and plenty of pepper. For the stuffing, mince the fillet of coley finely. Chop the ½ onion finely. Soak the bread roll in water and squeeze dry. Cook with the onion in the butter. Add to the minced coley. Stir in the egg and seasonings. Mix well. Fold in the soured cream, diced tongue, and chopped gherkins. Spread the stuffing over the eel fillets and roll up. Fasten with cocktail sticks.

For the liquor, place the head, bones, and skin of the eel, the sliced onion, prepared vegetables, and seasonings in lightly salted water and boil for 20 mins. Strain, and add the wine. Poach the eel rolls in the liquor for 30 mins. Take out with a draining spoon. Remove the cocktail sticks and leave to cool between two plates. Then cut each roll in half to make eight rolls. Bring 1 litre/1¾ pints/4½ cups of the liquor to the boil. Soak the gelatine and add to the hot liquid. Leave to gel. As soon as it begins to set, glaze the rolls with it.

Store in the refrigerator until needed. Arrange on a serving plate, and garnish with mayonnaise and parsley.

Spread the stuffing evenly over each fillet.

Glazed with aspic: garnished eel rolls.

Conger eel with herbs.

CONGER EEL WITH HERBS

Preparation time: 55 mins.
About 455 calories/1905 joules
Accompaniments: boiled potatoes, tossed in butter
and parsley

Metric/Imperial

1 fillet of conger eel,
  about 1kg/2¼ lbs
lemon juice
salt
1 onion
40g/1½ oz butter or
  margarine
250g/8 oz mushrooms
1 glass dry white wine
125ml/4 fl oz water
125ml/4 fl oz soured cream
1x15ml/1 tbs flour
pinch of sugar
3x15ml/3 tbs parsley,
  chopped
parsley and lemon slices
  to garnish

American

1 fillet of conger eel,
  about 2¼ lbs
lemon juice
salt
1 onion
3 tbs butter or
  margarine
½ lb mushrooms
1 glass dry white wine
½ cup water
½ cup sour cream
1 tbs flour
pinch of sugar
3 tbs parsley,
  chopped
parsley and lemon
  slices to garnish

Although this fish is known as conger eel it is in fact not a member of the eel family. It is really a kind of shark living in the North European seas.

Wash the fillet and pat dry. Cut in pieces. Sprinkle with salt and lemon juice. Dice the onion. Heat the butter or margarine in a wide saucepan and soften the onion in it. Chop the mushrooms coarsely and add to the onion, together with the fish. Sauté briefly. Pour in the wine and water. Cook gently for 20 mins. Remove the fish pieces and keep warm. Mix the flour with a little cold water and add to the fish liquor to thicken. Stir in the soured cream. Season with sugar and salt. Arrange the fish on a serving plate and sprinkle with chopped parsley. Pour over some of the sauce and serve the rest separately. Garnish with parsley and lemon slices.

Almond fish.

ALMOND FISH

Preparation time: 35 mins.
About 780 calories/3265 joules
Accompaniments: green salad and boiled rice

Metric/Imperial	American
4 fillets of white fish, each 250g/8 oz	4 fillets of white fish, each ½ lb
2x15ml/2 tbs lemon juice	2 tbs lemon juice
salt, white pepper	salt, white pepper
20g/¾ oz flour	1½ tbs flour
20g/¾ oz butter	1½ tbs butter
4 onions	4 onions
50g/2 oz butter	4 tbs butter
100g/4 oz flaked almonds	⅔ cup flaked almonds
125ml/4 fl oz soured cream	½ cup sour cream
125ml/4 fl oz cream	½ cup cream
lemon juice	lemon juice
few sprigs chives	few sprigs chives

Wash the fillets and pat dry. Sprinkle with lemon juice. Cover and leave for 15 mins. Pat dry again. Season with salt and pepper and roll in flour. Melt the butter in a small pan and sprinkle over the fish. Line a grill rack with greased foil. Place the fillets on it and cook under a preheated grill for 4 mins. each side.

In the meantime, chop the onions finely. Melt half the butter in a frying pan and soften the onions for 5 mins. Heat the remaining butter in a separate pan and fry the almonds until golden, around 5 mins. Add to the onions. Stir in the soured and fresh cream and heat. Season with salt, pepper, and lemon juice. Remove the fish from the grill and arrange on a heated serving plate. Pour the sauce over, and sprinkle with finely chopped chives.

Barbecued fish.

BARBECUED FISH

This warrants a separate paragraph. It is important to know which fish are suitable for grilling or barbecueing, and how to prepare them.

Small fish like herring, sole, mackerel, perch, and trout are ideal for grilling. Fillets of fish and fish cutlets are also delicious cooked on the barbecue.

Whole fish should be washed, gutted as usual, scaled if necessary, and carefully dried. Cut off heads and tails. Fillets should be just rinsed and dried. Sprinkle the fish inside and out (fillet on both sides) with lemon juice. Leave for 15 mins. to marinade. Season with salt. Then the fish or fish pieces should be brushed all over with oil, and lightly sprinkled with flour. Always oil the grill rack. Each fish or fillet could also be wrapped individually in greased aluminium foil. The piece of foil must be large enough to enclose the fish loosely. Grilling itself is easy; the important thing is to know the cooking times: herring, sole, mackerel, and trout need 4–7 mins. each side; fillets of fish need up to 5 mins. each side; fish cutlets need 6–8 mins. until they are cooked; fish wrapped in foil should be grilled for about 2 mins. longer.

It is, of course, not possible to give you the calorie content of barbecued fish, as there are so many different ways of cooking and serving it. For instance, placing a pat of butter on top will taste excellent, but will also increase the calorie content. Do not forget to sprinkle your barbecued fish with a little parsley.

Accompaniments: baked potatoes and grilled tomatoes; or crusty bread and a mixed salad.

MILLER'S WIFE FISH

Preparation time: 45 mins.
About 545 calories/2281 joules

A classic fish dish: miller's wife fish.

Metric/Imperial	American
1½kg/3½ lbs whole fish (plaice, tench, trout)	3½ lbs whole fish (plaice, tench, trout)
or 4 fillets of fish, each 200g/7 oz	or 4 fillets of fish, each 7 oz
juice 1 lemon	juice 1 lemon
salt	salt
4x15ml/4 tbs flour	4 tbs flour
4x15ml/4 tbs oil	4 tbs oil
few sprigs parsley	few sprigs parsley
1 lemon	1 lemon
1 small round lettuce	1 small round lettuce
40g/1½ oz butter	3 tbs butter

Gut whole fish, cut off head and fins (or ask the fishmonger to do it for you). Rinse the fish or fillets quickly under cold water and pat dry. Sprinkle with lemon juice and leave for 5 mins. Season with salt and roll in flour.

Heat the oil in a large frying pan. Fry the fish quickly for 1 min. on each side. Then lower the heat and cook fillets for a further 8 mins. on each side, or whole fish for 10 mins. until golden brown.

Meanwhile, chop half of the parsley finely, and leave the other half whole. Cut lemon into wedges. Remove the fish from the frying pan and arrange on a heated serving dish. Sprinkle with chopped parsley, and garnish with sprigs of parsley, lemon wedges, and lettuce leaves. Brown the butter quickly in a frying pan and pour over the fish.

A particularly interesting Chinese dish with excellent flavour: Chinese fish in soy sauce.

FISH IN SOY SAUCE

Preparation time without marinading: 50 mins.
About 465 calories/1946 joules
Accompaniment: boiled rice

Metric/Imperial

800g/1½ lbs haddock or
  cod
juice 1 lemon
For the fish marinade:
1x15ml/1 tbs soy sauce
1x15ml/1 tbs rice wine
  or sherry
salt, white pepper
pinch of powdered ginger

In addition:
250g/8 oz fillet of pork
1x5ml/1 tsp flour
For the meat marinade:
1x15ml/1 tbs soy sauce
1x15ml/1 tbs rice wine
  or sherry
1x5 ml/1 tsp flour
For the sauce:
2x15ml/2 tbs rice wine
  or sherry
2x15ml/2 tbs soy sauce
pinch of sugar, salt
125ml/4 fl oz stock
In addition:
6x15ml/6 tbs oil
1 piece preserved stem
  ginger
1 leek, sliced
100g/4 oz tinned bamboo
  shoots
150g/6 oz tinned button
  mushrooms

American

1½ lbs haddock or
  cod
juice 1 lemon

1 tbs soy sauce
1 tbs rice wine
  or sherry
salt, white pepper
pinch of powdered
  ginger

½ lb fillet of pork
1 tsp flour

1 tbs soy sauce
1 tbs sherry

1 tsp flour

2 tbs rice wine or
sherry
2 tbs soy sauce
pinch of sugar, salt
½ cup stock

6 tbs oil
1 piece preserved stem
  ginger
1 leek, sliced
4 oz canned bamboo
  shoots
6 oz canned
  mushrooms

All the ingredients that you need for this recipe are of course available in China. But this dish did not originate there. It was rather devised by one of the numerous Chinese chefs in America. It really tastes superb, and is less complicated to prepare than it might seem.

Rinse the fish, pat dry, and sprinkle with lemon juice.
Mix the ingredients for the fish marinade in a cup. Make several slashes across the back of the fish. Place in the bowl and pour the marinade over. Leave for 30 mins.

In the meantime, slice the fillet of pork in wafer thin slices. Roll in flour. Mix the ingredients for the meat marinade in a pan. Add the meat and stir occasionally.

For the sauce, mix the rice wine or sherry, soy sauce, sugar, and salt with the stock in a bowl.
Heat the oil in a sufficiently large saucepan. Add the roughly chopped stem ginger and the sliced leek. Cook for 5 mins. Remove from the pan. Place the fish in the pan and fry to 2 mins. each side until browned. Layer the bamboo shoots, drained mushrooms, leek, and ginger on top. Pour over the sauce, close the lid and heat until boiling. Reduce the heat and steam for about 15 mins. until cooked.

FILLETS OF FISH

There is no quicker or easier way to serve fish than by using fillets of fish. They are available ready prepared at fish counters or can be bought deep frozen. Fillets are obtained from fish caught in quantity like cod, haddock, and coley. To ensure the finest fillets, do not get any of the belly flaps.

If you prefer to buy the fish whole and cut your own fillets, the method is as follows: rinse the gutted fish under cold water. Cut off the head with a sharp knife and the fins with kitchen scissors. Make a cut along the backbone. With a flat fish like plaice or sole, make the cut along the natural markings in the centre of the fish, as the backbone lies underneath. To obtain the fillet, place a knife at an angle and lift off the flesh. With flat fish hold the knife sideways. You will now have two fillets. To skin them, hold the fillets with your left hand and separate the flesh with a sharp knife. Rinse under cold water and pat dry. They are now ready to be cooked.

1 Fillets are cut like this: make a cut in the back.

5 Pull off the skin on both sides like this.

2 Lift the flesh off with a knife held at an angle.

6 Now lift off the flesh sideways from the bones.

3 Separate the flesh from the skin with a knife.

7 Separate the fillet and remove the roe.

4 For flat fish, cut the skin behind the head.

FISH STEAKS MIAMI

Preparation time: 45 mins.
About 460 calories/1925 joules

Metric/Imperial	American
4 frozen fish steaks (white fish), each 200g/7 oz	4 frozen fish steaks (white fish), each 7 oz
juice 1 lemon	juice 1 lemon
salt	salt
4x15ml/4 tbs flour	4 tbs flour
50g/2 oz butter	4 tbs butter
4 tinned pineapple slices	4 canned pineapple slices
black pepper	black pepper
2 bananas	2 bananas
1x15ml/1 tbs paprika	1 tbs paprika
4x5ml/4 tsp mango chutney	4 tsp mango chutney
4 cocktail cherries	4 maraschino cherries
parsley for garnish	parsley for garnish
250g/8 oz tinned peaches	8 oz canned peaches

Sprinkle the frozen fish steaks with lemon juice and leave for 10 mins. Season with salt, and roll in flour. Melt the butter in a frying pan, and fry the fish steaks quickly for ½ min. on each side. Then cook for a further 5 mins. each side. Remove from the pan and arrange on a heated serving plate. Keep warm.

Drain the pineapple slices and season lightly with pepper. Peel and halve the bananas, and roll in paprika. Fry the fruit in the butter remaining in the frying pan for about 10 mins. Arrange on top of the fish steaks: pineapple slices in the centre and the halved bananas beside. Fill each hollow of the pineapple slices with mango chutney and a cherry. Garnish with sprigs of parsley.

Heat the peaches and their juice in the frying pan for 5 mins. and serve separately. Alternatively, place one peach half on top of each fish steak. Season the syrup with salt and pepper and serve separately.

TIP
Never defrost frozen fillets of fish. They should always be cooked from frozen, as otherwise the fish will become tasteless and lose its appearance. Always follow the instructions on the packet if they are bought fillets.

Fish steaks Miami.

FISH FILLETS IN WHITE WINE

Preparation time: 45 mins.
About 535 calories/2240 joules

Metric/Imperial	American
4 fish fillets weighing 200g/6 oz each, fresh or frozen	4 fish fillets weighing 6 oz each, fresh or frozen
juice 1 lemon, salt	juice 1 lemon, salt
250ml/8 fl oz white wine	1 cup white wine
250ml/8 fl oz water	1 cup water
few sprigs parsley	few sprigs parsley
1 punnet of mustard and cress	1 punnet of cress
1x5ml/1 tsp dried dill	1 tsp dried dill
margarine	margarine
50g/2 oz butter	¼ cup butter
1 onion	1 onion
25g/1 oz flour	2 tbs flour
1 egg yolk	1 egg yolk
white pepper	white pepper
100g/4 oz button mushrooms	1 cup mushrooms
2x15ml/2 tbs dried breadcrumbs	2 tbs dried breadcrumbs
4x15ml/4 tbs Emmenthal cheese, grated	4 tbs Swiss cheese, grated
25g/1 oz butter	2 tbs butter
For the tomato sauce:	
1x15ml/1 tbs butter	1 tbs butter
1x15ml/1 tbs flour	1 tbs flour
½ clove garlic, salt	½ clove garlic, salt
150g/5 oz tomato puree	⅔ cup tomato paste
250ml/8 fl oz chicken stock	1¼ cups chicken stock
few sprigs parsley	few sprigs parsley
1 lemon	1 lemon

FISH FONDUE

Preparation time: 30 mins. — cooking is done by guests
About 885 calories/3705 joules
Accompaniments: plenty of crusty bread, mixed or green salad, tomato ketchup, chutneys, pickled gherkins, mixed pickles, marinaded red peppers, olives, lemon wedges, and various commercial sauces. Serve with plenty of white or rosé wine.

Metric/Imperial	American
1 kg/2¼ lb thick fillets of fish	2¼ lb thick fillets of fish
juice 2 lemons	juice 2 lemons
For the fondue sauces:	
200ml/7 fl oz mayonnaise	1 cup mayonnaise
2x5ml/2 tsp mustard	2 tsp hot mustard
salt, white pepper	salt, white pepper
sugar, single cream	sugar, light cream
2x15ml/2 tbs tomato ketchup	2 tbs tomato ketchup
1x15ml/1 tbs barbecue sauce	1 tbs barbecue sauce
1x15ml/1 tbs paprika	1 tbs paprika
3x5ml/3 tsp curry powder	3 tsp curry powder
125ml/4 fl oz whipping cream	½ cup whipping cream
4x5ml/4 tsp creamed horseradish	4 tsp creamed horseradish
few sprigs parsley for garnish	few sprigs parsley for garnish
oil for the fondue	oil for the fondue

Fondue cooked with meat is quite well known. But have you tried fish fondue? Served with several savoury sauces and other delicacies, it really is a delicious way of serving fish.

Rinse the fillets, pat dry, sprinkle with lemon juice, and leave for a few mins.

In the meantime, prepare the sauces. Divide the mayonnaise into 4 portions. For the first sauce: mix the mayonnaise with mustard, salt, pepper, a pinch of sugar, and some single cream. Season well.

For the second sauce: mix the mayonnaise with tomato ketchup, barbecue sauce, salt, pepper, a pinch of sugar, and some single cream.

For the third sauce: mix the mayonnaise with paprika, salt, pepper, 1x5ml/1 tsp sugar, and single cream until smooth. Season well.

For the fourth sauce: mix the mayonnaise with curry powder, salt, pepper, a pinch of sugar, and some single cream. Season well.

For the fifth sauce: whip the whipping cream until it holds it shape and fold in the creamed horseradish. Season well with salt, pepper, and a pinch of sugar. Add more horseradish to taste.

Pour the sauces in individual small bowls and arranged around the fondue set.

Pat the fillets of fish until quite dry. They must not be damp as the moisture might splatter when being cooked. Cut the fillets into even-sized cubes. Place on the serving dish and garnish with parsley.

Heat enough oil (about half full) in the fondue pot on the cooker. When quite hot set over the lighted burner. Serve with the suggested accompaniments.

Preheat oven to 180°C/350°F/Gas 4. Rinse the fish fillets under cold water and pat dry. Sprinkle with lemon juice and leave to marinade for 10 mins. Season with salt.

Heat the white wine, water, chopped parsley, cress and dill in a saucepan and poach the fish in the liquid for 10 mins. Remove the fish with a slotted spoon. Grease an ovenproof dish with the margarine and place the fish fillets inside. Melt the butter in a frying pan and fry the finely chopped onion until golden. Pour in the fish liquor and simmer for 7 mins. Beat the egg yolk with a little of the liquor, then stir back into the sauce. Heat but don't boil. Season with salt and pepper. Add the mushrooms and spread the sauce over the fish. Sprinkle with the breadcrumbs and grated Emmenthal cheese. Dot with flakes of butter and place in the preheated oven on the centre shelf for 10 mins.

For the sauce, melt the butter and stir in the flour. Crush the garlic with a little salt and add to the mixture. Stir in the tomato puree and stock. Whisk until the sauce is smooth and simmer for 7 mins. Taste for seasoning.

Arrange the fish fillets on a heated serving dish and garnish with parsley and lemon wedges. Spoon a little of the tomato sauce over and serve the rest separately.

Delicious sauces and various accompaniments for the fish fondue.

FISHBALLS IN CRAYFISH SAUCE

Preparation time: 55 mins.
About 610 calories/2553 joules

Metric/Imperial

For the fishballs:
1kg/2¼ lbs fillets of white fish
juice 1 lemon
4 onions, sliced
50g/2 oz butter or margarine
1 leek
2 bread rolls soaked in water
salt, paprika
white pepper
2 eggs
5x15ml/5 tbs dried breadcrumbs
2 litres/3½ pints water
For the sauce:
40g/1½ oz butter
25g/1 oz flour
375ml/12 fl oz fish liquor
4x15ml/4 tbs cream, salt
2x15ml/2 tbs butter (crayfish butter, if available)
100g/4 oz crayfish tails
dill leaves for garnish

American

2¼ lbs fillets of white fish
juice 1 lemon
4 onions, sliced
4 tbs butter or margarine
1 leek
2 bread rolls soaked in water
salt, paprika
white pepper
2 eggs
5 tbs dried breadcrumbs
9 cups water

3 tbs butter
2 tbs flour
1½ cups fish liquor
4 tbs cream, salt
2 tbs butter (crayfish butter, if available)
¼ lb crayfish tails
dill leaves for garnish

For the fishballs, wash the fillet and pat dry. Sprinkle with lemon juice. Melt the butter in a frying pan and fry the sliced onions until golden. Trim the leek, wash, and cut in pieces. Cube the fish fillet. Mince finely together with the cooled onion, leek, and soaked and squeezed bread rolls. Place in a bowl and add seasonings. Stir in the eggs and dried breadcrumbs and mix well. Heat the water and add salt. Using two tablespoons dipped in cold water, make small balls. Place in the simmering water. Reduce the heat and poach gently for 15 mins. Do not boil! Take out with a draining spoon and arrange in a serving bowl. Keep warm.

For the sauce, melt the butter in a saucepan. Stir in the flour. Add the fish liquor and stir vigorously with a wire whisk. Cook for 5 mins. and then remove from the heat. Stir in the cream and season with salt. Add the crayfish butter and let it melt in the sauce. Add the crayfish tails and heat gently, but do not allow to boil. Pour the sauce over the fishballs and garnish with dill leaves.

Fishballs in crayfish sauce.

FISH GOULASH

Preparation time: 45 mins.
About 385 calories/1612 joules
Accompaniments: seasonal salad and rice or
boiled potatoes

Metric/Imperial	American
2 onions	2 onions
1 clove garlic	1 clove garlic
salt	salt
50g/2 oz streaky bacon	2 fatty bacon slices
2x15ml/2 tbs oil	2 tbs oil
3x15ml/3 tbs tomato purée	3 tbs tomato paste
250ml/8 fl oz white wine	1 cup white wine
375ml/12 fl oz hot stock	1½ cups hot stock
4 tomatoes	4 tomatoes
salt, white pepper	salt, white pepper
few sprigs parsley, chopped	½ cup chopped parsley
2x5ml/2 tsp paprika	2 tsp paprika
750g/1½ lbs fresh or frozen fillets of fish	1½ lbs fresh or frozen fillets of fish
juice 1 lemon	juice 1 lemon
25g/1 oz flour	2 tbs flour

Chop the onions coarsely. Crush the garlic with a little salt. Mix together. Dice the bacon and heat in a saucepan until the fat runs. Fry the onions and garlic briefly. Add the oil, heat, and stir in the tomato purée. Pour in the white wine and hot stock. Simmer gently. Skin the tomatoes and chop finely. Add to the sauce. Season with salt and pepper. Add chopped parsley and paprika. Mix well and simmer gently. Sprinkle the fish fillet with lemon juice. After 5 mins. cut in large pieces. Season with salt. Add the fish to the sauce and cook gently for 15 mins. After 10 mins. thicken the sauce with the flour mixed with a little water.

TIP
The many bones of flat fish are more easily removed if the head is placed to the left and the belly opening to the front of the plate.

Russian flounder fillets.

RUSSIAN FLOUNDER FILLETS

Preparation time: 45 mins.
About 455 calories/1904 joules

Metric/Imperial	American
750g/1½ lbs fillets of flounder	1½ lbs fillets of flounder
juice 1 lemon	juice 1 lemon
salt, white pepper	salt, white pepper
25g/1 oz butter	2 tbs butter
4x15ml/4 tbs dried breadcrumbs	4 tbs dried breadcrumbs
1 large onion	1 large onion
250ml/8 fl oz cream	1 cup cream
For the garnish:	
chopped parsley or dill	chopped parsley or dill

The flounder, a tasty flat fish, is a near relative of the sole. Flounders are found mainly in the North Sea and the Baltic, but sometimes they swim inland up the rivers. They are usually prepared like soles. Incidentally, they are slightly bigger than soles and have rough scales. Flounder is at its best from October until December.
Wash the fish and pat dry. Sprinkle on both sides with lemon juice. Leave for 15 mins. Season with salt and pepper. Melt the butter in a large frying pan and lightly fry the breadcrumbs. Finely dice the onion and fry until golden. Stir in the cream. Season with salt and pepper. Cut each fillet in three and place over the breadcrumb mixture. Cover and cook gently for 15 mins. Arrange on a serving plate, and garnish with chopped parsley or dill.

FRIED FLOUNDER

Preparation time: 35 mins.
About 475 calories/1988 joules
Accompaniments: boiled potatoes tossed in melted butter and parsley, or potato salad

Metric/Imperial	American
1kg/2¼ lbs flounder, ready gutted	**2¼ lbs flounder, ready gutted**
juice 1 lemon	**juice 1 lemon**
salt, white pepper	**salt, white pepper**
5x15ml/5 tbs flour	**5 tbs flour**
8x15ml/8 tbs oil	**8 tbs oil**
For the garnish:	
parsley	**parsley**
1 lemon	**1 lemon**

Scale if necessary, rinse, and pat dry. Sprinkle inside and out with lemon juice. Leave for 10 mins. Season with salt and pepper and roll in flour. Heat the oil in a large frying pan and fry the flounder gently for 10 mins. each side. Arrange on a preheated plate, garnish with chopped parsley and lemon wedges.

HADDOCK

The haddock is a member of the cod family. This fish, with its greyish brown back, silvery sides, and black line along its side, is particularly flavoursome. It tastes nice poached with butter, with mustard sauce, or horseradish sauce, and also shallow or deep fried.

Haddock is caught by trawling net in the North Sea and the North Atlantic. It looks very like cod but, when buying, haddock can be recognized by the dark spot above the breast fin.

KEUFTA

Preparation time: 40 mins.
About 295 calories/1235 joules

Metric/Imperial	American
500g/1 lb potatoes	**1 lb potatoes**
750g/1½ lbs fillets of haddock	**1½ lbs fillets of haddock**
2 onions	**2 onions**
3 eggs	**3 eggs**
white and black pepper	**white and black pepper**
parsley, chopped	**parsley, chopped**
1 litre/1¾ pints oil for frying	**4½ cups oil for frying**

Peel the potatoes and cook in boiling, salted water for 20 mins. Drain, let excess steam escape, and cool. Wash and skin the haddock. Mash together the potatoes and fish, or purée in an electric mixer. Dice the onions finely, and add to the mixture. Season with salt and pepper and add the eggs. Mix well and stir in chopped parsley to taste. Heat the oil in a deep saucepan or deep fat fryer to 180°C/350°F. Shape the fish mixture into balls of 5cm/2 in. diameter. Fry in the hot oil for 8 mins. Do not crowd the pan. Take out with a draining spoon, drain, and arrange on a preheated serving dish. Keep warm until all fish balls are cooked then serve immediately.

An example of oriental cuisine: Keufta (fish balls).

Haddock with herbs.

HADDOCK WITH HERBS

Preparation time: 1 hr.
About 225 calories/941 joules
Accompaniments: green salad and potatoes tossed in
butter and parsley

Metric/Imperial	American
750g/1½ lbs fillets of haddock	1½ lbs fillets of haddock
juice 1 lemon	juice 1 lemon
salt	salt
3 onions	3 onions
500g/1 lb button mushrooms	1 lb mushrooms
40g/1½ oz margarine	3 tbs margarine
white pepper	white pepper
few sprigs each dill, chives and parsley	few sprigs each dill, chives and parsley
butter or margarine for greasing	butter or margarine
125ml/4 fl oz white wine	½ cup white wine
2x15ml/2 tbs dried breadcrumbs	2 tbs dried breadcrumbs
40g/1½ oz butter	3 tbs butter
For the garnish:	
1 tomato	1 tomato
2 sprigs parsley	2 sprigs parsley

Preheat oven to 220°C/425°F/Gas 7. Wash the haddock and pat dry. Sprinkle with lemon juice, cover, and leave for 10 mins.

Cut the fillet in four pieces and sprinkle both sides with a little salt. Dice the onions. Wipe, trim, and slice the mushrooms, leaving very small ones whole. Melt the margarine in a frying pan and fry the onions and mushrooms for 5 mins. Season well with salt and pepper. Chop parsley, and finely snip dill and chives. Stir the herbs into the onions and mushrooms. Grease an ovenproof dish with butter or margarine. Spread half the onion and mushroom mixture on the bottom of the dish. Place the fish fillets on top and cover with the remaining mixture. Pour over the white wine, sprinkle with breadcrumbs, and dot with butter.

Place in the preheated oven on the centre shelf for 25 mins. Garnish with quarters of tomato and sprigs of parsley.

HADDOCK WITH PEPPERS

Preparation time: 45 mins.
About 305 calories/1276 joules

Metric/Imperial	American
750g/1½ lbs fillets of haddock	1½ lbs fillets of haddock
juice 1 lemon	juice 1 lemon
salt	salt
1 onion	1 onion
1 red and 1 green pepper	1 red and 1 green pepper
2 tomatoes	2 tomatoes
40g/1½ oz margarine	2 tbs margarine
125ml/4 fl oz stock	½ cup stock
5x15ml/5 tbs white wine	5 tbs white wine
4x15ml/4 tbs cream	4 tbs cream
4x15ml/1 tbs flour	1 tbs flour
1x5ml/1 tsp paprika	1 tsp paprika
salt, white pepper	salt, white pepper
chopped dill	chopped dill

Wash the haddock and pat dry. Sprinkle with lemon juice and leave for 10 mins. Season with salt. Dice the onion, deseed the peppers and cut in strips. Skin and slice the tomatoes. Melt the margarine in a saucepan. Fry the diced onion gently for 3 mins. Add the peppers and cook for 5 mins., stirring occasionally. Add the tomatoes, stock, and wine. Carefully place the fish in the saucepan, cover, and poach gently for 15 mins. Remove the fish and arrange on a preheated serving plate. Cover and keep warm. Bring the fish liquor to the boil. Mix the cream with the flour, paprika, salt, and pepper. Add to the liquor and cook for 3 mins. Pour the sauce over the fish fillets. Sprinkle with chopped dill and serve.

The flesh of the haddock is particularly flavoursome and mixes well with the aromatic taste of peppers.

HADDOCK WITH GRAPES

Preparation time: 40 mins.
About 405 calories/1695 joules
Accompaniments: peas and boiled potatoes, tossed in butter and parsley

Metric/Imperial	American
750g/1½ lbs fillets of haddock	1½ lbs fillets of haddock
juice 1 lemon	juice 1 lemon
salt	salt
40g/1½ oz margarine	3 tbs margarine
125ml/4 fl oz white wine	½ cup white wine
250g/8 oz white grapes	½ lb white grapes
For the sauce:	
125ml/4 fl oz cream	½ cup cream
2x15ml/2 tbs flour	2 tbs flour
2x15ml/2 tbs orange juice	2 tbs orange juice
salt, white pepper	salt, white pepper

Wash the haddock and pat dry. Sprinkle with lemon juice. Cover and leave for 15 mins. Season with salt. Melt the margarine in a large frying pan. Fry the fish for 3 mins. on one side. Add the white wine and cover. Poach gently for 15 mins.

Wash and halve the grapes and remove any pips. Spread over the fish. Cover the pan again and cook for a further 5 mins. Carefully take out the fish and grapes and place on a heated serving dish. Cover and keep warm.

For the sauce, mix the flour with the cream. Boil up the cooking liquor and stir in the cream mixture. Cook for 3 mins. Add orange juice and seasoning. Pour the sauce over the fish and serve.

HADDOCK WITH VEGETABLES

Gestofde Schelvis

Preparation time: 50 mins.
About 235 calories/983 joules
Accompaniments: mashed potatoes or potato salad

Metric/Imperial	American
750g/1½ lbs fillets of haddock	1½ lbs fillets of haddock
juice 1 lemon	juice 1 lemon
salt, white pepper	salt, white pepper
grated nutmeg	grated nutmeg
butter for greasing	butter for greasing
1 lemon	1 lemon
200g/7 oz each cauliflower, peas, carrots, and celery	scant ½ lb each cauliflower, peas, carrots, and celery
2 onions	2 onions
2 rusks	2 rusks
125ml/4 fl oz hot stock	½ cup hot stock
25g/1 oz butter	2 tbs butter
6x15ml/6 tbs white wine	6 tbs white wine

Haddock cooked this way is a Dutch speciality, which is very easy to prepare.

Preheat oven to 220°C/425°F/Gas 7. Wash the haddock and pat dry. Sprinkle with lemon juice and leave for 10 mins. Then season on both sides with salt, pepper, and grated nutmeg. Grease an ovenproof dish with butter. Place the fish inside. Peel the lemon, remove all the white pith, and cut in thin slices. Remove pips and place on top of the fish.

Blanch the cauliflower, carrots, peas, and celery in a saucepan of boiling water for 5 mins. Drain.

Chop the onions roughly, and mince finely with the other vegetables or purée in an electric mixer. Spread over the fish. Crush the rusks finely and sprinkle over the vegetables. Pour the stock into a saucepan. Stir in the butter and heat. Then add the wine. Pour over the fish and vegetables. Place the dish in the preheated oven on the centre shelf for 20 mins.

BAKED GARNISHED HADDOCK

Psari Plaki

Preparation time: 55 mins.
About 582 calories/2436 joules
Accompaniments: mixed salad and potatoes tossed in butter and parsley

Metric/Imperial	American
1 whole haddock, about 1.5kg/3½ lbs (cod may be substituted)	1 whole haddock, about 3½ lbs (cod may be substituted)
juice 1 lemon	juice 1 lemon
1x5ml/1 tsp salt	1 tsp salt
1x5ml/1 tsp oregano	1 tsp oregano
black pepper	black pepper
3x15ml/3 tbs olive oil	3 tbs olive oil
4 shallots	4 shallots
2 cloves garlic	2 cloves garlic
5x15ml/5 tbs dried breadcrumbs	5 tbs dried breadcrumbs
salt	salt
60g/2¼ oz butter, melted	4 tbs butter, melted
few sprigs parsley	few sprigs parsley
350g/12 oz tomatoes	¾ lb tomatoes
1 lemon	1 lemon
1 onion	1 onion
1x15ml/1 tbs butter	1 tbs butter

Preheat oven to 180°C/350°F/Gas 4. For this Greek dish, scale, gut, and rinse the fish. Sprinkle inside and out with lemon juice and leave to soak. Make 3 1–2½cm/½–1 in. cuts in the back of the fish. Mix salt, oregano, and black pepper and rub into the slits. Grease an ovenproof dish with ⅔ rds oil. Place fish inside and sprinkle with remaining oil. Chop the shallots and garlic very finely. Mix with the dried breadcrumbs, salt, and melted butter. Spread over the fish. Chop the parsley and sprinkle over the dish. Wash tomatoes and make crosswise cuts into the top. Place beside the fish. Slice the lemon and make a cut to the centre, twist, and lay on top of the fish. Cut the onion into rings. Brown in the butter and add to the fish. Cover and place in the preheated oven for 30 mins.

Psari Plaki: garnished haddock from Greece.

HAKE

The hake, a relative of the cod, is a fish of prey. Its favourite food is young mackerel, young herring, sardines, and similar small fish. The main fishing grounds are the west and southwest coasts of the European Atlantic. But it is also caught in the north as far as Iceland and northern Norway, the North Sea, the Mediterranean, and in the waters of West Africa.

Because of its slim build, it bears great resemblance to its freshwater cousin, the pike. Hake can reach a length of 1m/3 ft and weigh up to 10kg/22 lbs. Its commercial size is about 61–76cm/2–2½ ft.

HAKE LEOPOLD

Preparation time: 1 hr. 35 mins.
About 535 calories/2239 joules

Metric/Imperial	American
8 fillets of hake, each 100g/4 oz	8 fillets of hake, each 4 oz
juice 1 lemon	juice 1 lemon
salt	salt
For the fish liquor:	
250ml/8 fl oz white wine	1 cup white wine
250ml/8 fl oz water	1 cup water
1 onion	1 onion
2 cloves	2 cloves
½ bay leaf	½ bay leaf
3 peppercorns	3 peppercorns
2½ml/½ tsp salt	½ tsp salt
For the Geneva sauce:	
1 carrot, 1 onion, 1 stick celery	1 carrot, 1 onion, 1 stick celery
25g/1 oz margarine	2 tbs margarine
15g/½ oz flour	1 tbs flour
125ml/4 fl oz red wine	½ cup red wine
125ml/4 fl oz fish liquor	½ cup fish liquor
1x15ml/1 tsp anchovy paste	1 tsp anchovy paste
15g/½ oz butter	1 tbs butter
For the white wine sauce:	
125ml/4 fl oz fish liquor	½ cup fish liquor
cayenne pepper	cayenne pepper
1x15ml/1 tsp cornflour	1 tsp cornstarch
125ml/4 fl oz white wine	½ cup white wine
1 egg yolk	1 egg yolk
50g/2 oz butter	2 tbs butter
125g/4 oz prawns	4 oz shrimps
2x5ml/2 tsp lemon juice	2 tsp lemon juice
In addition:	
200g/7 oz tin lobster soup	7 oz can lobster soup
175g/6 oz tinned lobster	1 cup canned lobster
1x5ml/1 tsp cornflour	1 tsp cornstarch
25g/1 oz tinned truffles	1 oz canned truffles

Rinse the fillets of hake and pat dry. Sprinkle with lemon juice and leave for 10 mins. Season with salt. For the fish liquor, put white wine, water, the onion spiked with cloves and bay leaf, peppercorns, and salt in large pan and bring to the boil. Insert the fish, and poach gently for 10 mins. Do not let it boil. Lift out carefully, drain, and place on a heated serving plate. Cover, and keep warm. Strain the fish liquor.

For the Geneva sauce, wash, trim, and finely dice the vegetables. Melt the margarine in a saucepan, and fry them until lightly browned. Sprinkle with flour, and cook for about 5 mins. until a good dark colour. Pour in the red wine and fish liquor. Simmer for 8 mins. Rub through a strainer, and season with anchovy paste. Heat gently and whisk in the butter. Cover, and keep warm.

For the white wine sauce, heat the fish liquor. Season with cayenne pepper. Mix the cornflour with the white wine, and add to the liquor. Bring to the boil and cook until thickened. Mix the egg yolk with a little sauce and add. Stir in half of the butter. Drain the prawns. Melt the remaining butter in a frying pan and fry prawns for 2 mins. Sprinkle with lemon juice and add to the sauce. Keep warm.

Heat the lobster soup according to instructions on the tin. Mix the cornflour with a little water and stir into the soup. Bring to the boil, and remove from the heat.

Drain the lobster meat, and remove any bits of chitin. Flake with a fork. Chop the truffles roughly. Garnish the hake: 4 fillets should be covered with lobster sauce, and sprinkled with chopped truffles. Cover the remaining fillets with Geneva sauce and sprinkle the lobster meat on top. Pour the white wine sauce around the fish.

HAKE IN FOIL

Preparation time: 1 hr. 10 mins.
About 280 calories/1172 joules

Metric/Imperial

1 hake, about 1kg/2¼ lbs,
  ready prepared
juice 1 lemon
For the stuffing:
½ stale bread roll
5x15ml/5 tbs milk
40g/1½oz butter
1 onion, finely diced
100g/4 oz button
  mushrooms
few sprigs parsley
1 egg
salt, white pepper
grated nutmeg
butter for greasing
125ml/4 fl oz white wine
For the garnish:
few sprigs parsley
1 lemon

American

1 hake, about 2¼ lbs,
  ready prepared
juice 1 lemon

½ stale bread roll
5 tbs milk
3 tbs butter
1 onion, finely diced
4 oz mushrooms

few sprigs parsley
1 egg
salt, white pepper
grated nutmeg
butter for greasing
½ cup white wine

few sprigs parsley
1 lemon

Preheat oven to 200°C/400°F/Gas 6. Wash the hake and pat dry. Sprinkle with lemon juice and leave for 15 mins.
Meanwhile, soak bread roll in milk for the stuffing. Melt butter in a frying pan. Fry the onion for 7 mins. until golden. Add the finely sliced button mushrooms and cook for 3 mins., stirring occasionally.Chop the parsley. Beat the egg in a bowl. Add the soaked and squeezed bread roll. Mix to a firm paste with the onion, mushrooms, and parsley. Season well with salt, pepper, and grated nutmeg. Stuff the hake with the mixture, and fasten the opening with cocktail sticks. Rub the fish all over with salt. Grease a large sheet of aluminium foil with butter and loosely wrap the fish in it. Seal the ends tightly. Pour the white wine in the top opening and seal that, too. Place the hake on a rack in the centre of the preheated oven for 30 mins. Arrange the fish in the opened foil on a heated serving plate and garnish with sprigs of parsley and slices of lemon.

Hake Leopold: an extravagant fish recipe of international cuisine. Lobster and truffles make it irresistible.

HALIBUT

The halibut is the largest flat fish we know. It is also one of the tastiest sea fish in our waters, and is valued for its high content of vitamins, nutrients, and minerals. It is available raw—when it is best poached, fried, or grilled—or smoked.

HALIBUT WITH CONCASSE TOMATOES

Preparation time: 30 mins.
About 505 calories/2113 joules
Accompaniments: buttered potatoes with parsley and green salad

Metric/Imperial	American
500g/1 lb tomatoes	1 lb tomatoes
4 shallots or 2 onions	4 shallots or 2 onions
25g/1 oz butter	2 tbs butter
salt, white pepper	salt, white pepper
4 halibut steaks, each 250g/8 oz	4 halibut steaks, each ½ lb
garlic salt	garlic salt
25g/1 oz flour	2 tbs flour
4x15ml/4 tbs oil for frying	4 tbs oil for frying
few sprigs parsley, chopped	few sprigs parsley, chopped

Concasse tomatoes is a special cooking term and means, literally, melted tomatoes. Accompanying halibut, as in this recipe, it is easy to prepare and looks pretty.

Skin, seed, and chop the tomatoes roughly. Dice the shallots or onions.

Melt the butter in a saucepan and fry the shallots until golden. Add the tomatoes. Season and simmer gently for 7 mins. Some of the liquid should evaporate.

In the meantime, wash the halibut steaks and pat dry. Rub in salt and garlic salt. Roll in flour. Heat the oil in a frying pan and fry the steaks for 6 mins. on each side. Arrange the cooked halibut steaks on a heated serving dish. Cover with *concasse tomatoes* and sprinkle with chopped parsley.

Halibut with concasse tomatoes is a quickly prepared dish any cook could be proud of.

Halibut in tomato sauce.

HALIBUT IN TOMATO SAUCE

Preparation time: 1 hr. 40 mins.
About 570 calories/2386 joules

Metric/Imperial

4 halibut cutlets,
   each 200g/7 oz
juice 1 lemon
250g/8 oz onions
2 carrots
1 large parsley stalk
500g/1 lb tomatoes
1 bay leaf
1 litre/1⅓ pints water
salt
75g/3 oz butter
50g/2 oz button
   mushrooms
25g/1 oz flour
125ml/4 fl oz cream
1x15ml/1 tbs capers
50g/2 oz green olives

American

4 halibut cutlets,
   each 7 oz
juice 1 lemon
½ lb onions
2 carrots
1 large parsley stalk
1 lb tomatoes
1 bay leaf
4½ cups water
salt
6 tbs butter
1 cup mushrooms

2 tbs flour
½ cup cream
1 tbs capers
⅓ cup green olives

Wash halibut cutlets and pat dry. Sprinkle with lemon juice and leave aside. Slice onions, and chop carrots and parsley stalk roughly. Place with skinned and chopped tomatoes and a bay leaf in a saucepan of boiling water. Stir in salt and 40g/ 1½ oz/3 tbs butter. Boil rapidly for 5 mins., stirring constantly. Reduce heat and simmer for 30 mins. Rub through a strainer and return to saucepan. Sprinkle fish with salt and add to sauce. Bring to the boil and reduce heat immediately. Poach for 8 mins. Take out the cutlets and arrange on a serving dish. Cover and keep warm.

Reheat the sauce and boil for about 15 mins. until reduced to half. Trim the mushrooms and fry in the remaining butter for 5 mins. until cooked. Season with salt. Stir in the flour. Add the tomato sauce, then take off the heat and stir in the cream. Add the drained capers and halved and stoned olives. Season and pour over the fish.

Poached halibut.

POACHED HALIBUT

Preparation time: 40 mins.
About 755 calories/3160 joules

Metric/Imperial	American
1 whole halibut, or a piece weighing 1½kg/ 2–3 lbs	1 whole halibut, or a piece weighing 2–3 lbs
For the marinade:	
1 litre/1¾ pints water	4½ cups water
juice 1 lemon	juice 1 lemon
For the fish liquor:	
2 litres/3½ pints water	9 cups water
250ml/8 fl oz white wine	1 cup white wine
1 onion	1 onion
1 bay leaf	1 bay leaf
5 peppercorns, salt	5 peppercorns, salt
150g/5 oz butter	⅔ cup butter

The smallest halibut weigh 3–4 lbs, but they are not always available whole. If you cannot get one, buy a large piece weighing about 1½kg/2–3 lbs. A whole fish, however, is more juicy.

Rinse the halibut under cold water inside and out. Scale if necessary. Marinade in water and lemon juice while preparing the fish liquor. In a large saucepan, bring to the boil the water, white wine, halved onion, bay leaf, peppercorns, and salt. Add the fish and poach gently for 15 mins. When you can pull out the fin on the back quite easily, the fish is cooked.

Meanwhile, melt the butter until browned. Remove the whey. Arrange the fish on a heated serving plate and pour over the brown butter.

HALIBUT WITH CAPERS

Preparation time: 25 mins.
About 415 calories/1737 joules
Accompaniments: green salad and mashed potatoes

Halibut with capers.

Metric/Imperial	American
4 halibut steaks, each 250g/8 oz	4 halibut steaks, each ½ lb
salt, celery salt	salt, celery salt
4x15ml/4 tbs flour	4 tbs flour
50g/2 oz butter	4 tbs butter
4x15ml/4 tbs capers	4 tbs capers
juice 1 lemon	juice 1 lemon
2½ml/½ tsp sugar	½ tsp sugar

Wash the halibut steaks and pat dry. Rub with salt and celery salt. Roll in flour. Melt butter in a frying pan. Fry the fish steaks for 5 mins. each side on medium heat (not too hot, as the butter might burn). Remove the steaks, place on a heated serving dish, and keep warm. Drain the capers, and stir into the butter with the lemon juice and sugar. Pour over the fish and serve.

TIP
Should one eat the skin of the halibut? Fish gourmets say it should be eaten whenever the fish is served fried.

HALIBUT STEAKS WITH LEMON SAUCE

Preparation time: 55 mins.
About 515 calories/2155 joules
Accompaniments: tomato salad and boiled rice

Metric/Imperial	American
2 large halibut steaks, each 400g/14 oz	2 large halibut steaks, each 14 oz
salt, black pepper	salt, black pepper
oil for greasing	oil for greasing
2 tomatoes	2 tomatoes
1 onion	1 onion
60g/2½ oz butter	5 tbs butter
60g/2½ oz fresh white breadcrumbs	5 tbs fresh white breadcrumbs
1x15ml/1 tbs parsley, chopped	1 tbs parsley, chopped
125ml/4 fl oz boiling water	½ cup boiling water
For the sauce:	
125ml/4 fl oz lemon juice	½ cup lemon juice
grated rind ½ lemon	grated rind ½ lemon
white pepper	white pepper
100g/4 oz mayonnaise	½ cup mayonnaise
For the garnish:	
1 lemon	1 lemon
paprika	paprika

Preheat oven to 200°C/400°F/Gas 6. Wash the halibut steaks and pat dry. Rub one side of one steak with salt and pepper. Grease an ovenproof dish with oil. Put in the steak seasoned side down. Skin and chop the tomatoes, and chop the onion finely. Melt ⅓ of the butter in a saucepan, stir in the breadcrumbs, tomatoes, onion, and parsley. Season with salt and pepper. Spread the mixture on top of the fish in the dish. Place the second steak on top, season, dot with butter. Pour in boiling water and place in the preheated oven on the centre shelf for 30 mins.

For the sauce, mix the lemon juice and rind with the mayonnaise and pepper in a bowl. Place the bowl over a saucepan of hot water and heat gently. Do not boil. Place the fish on a heated serving plate and garnish with lemon slices and paprika. Serve the lemon sauce separately.

HALIBUT IN ORANGE SAUCE

Preparation time: 60 mins.
About 475 calories/1988 joules

Metric/Imperial	American
4 halibut steaks, each 250g/8 oz	4 halibut steaks, each ½ lb
1 clove garlic, salt	1 clove garlic, salt
2x15ml/2 tbs parsley, chopped	2 tbs parsley, chopped
white pepper	white pepper
6x15ml/6 tbs dried breadcrumbs	6 tbs dried breadcrumbs
oil for greasing	oil for greasing
500ml/16 fl oz freshly squeezed orange juice	2 cups freshly pressed orange juice
50g/2 oz butter	4 tbs butter
1 orange for garnish	1 orange for garnish

Halibut in orange sauce.

Preheat oven to 180°C/350°F/Gas 4. Wash the halibut steaks and pat dry. Crush the garlic with salt. Rub into the fish. Sprinkle with parsley, salt, and pepper. Roll in breadcrumbs. Grease a shallow ovenproof dish. Put in the fish and pour over the orange juice. Dot with butter. Cover and place in the preheated oven on the centre shelf for 20 mins. Meanwhile, peel the orange, remove all pith, and slice. When the fish steaks are cooked, arrange on a heated serving plate. Pour over the liquor and garnish with slices of orange.

HALIBUT WITH BUTTON MUSHROOMS

Preparation time: 1 hr. 5 mins.
About 455 calories/1904 joules

Metric/Imperial	American
500g/1 lb potatoes	1 lb potatoes
4 halibut steaks, each 250g/8 oz	4 halibut steaks, each ½ lb
salt, white pepper	salt, white pepper
juice ½ lemon	juice ½ lemon
2x15ml/2 tbs butter	2 tbs butter
175g/6 oz button mushrooms	6 oz mushrooms
125ml/4 fl oz white wine	½ cup white wine
For the garnish:	
2 hardboiled eggs	2 hardboiled eggs
parsley	parsley

Preheat oven to 220°C/425°F/Gas 7. Peel potatoes, cut into medium-sized pieces, and boil in salted water for 15 mins. Drain. Wash the halibut steaks and pat dry. Season and sprinkle with lemon juice. Cut 4 large pieces of aluminium foil and spread butter thickly on each. Place the fish on top and fold up the edges of the foil. Divide mushrooms and potatoes between the four, and pour a portion of wine over each. Seal the foil parcels well. Place in the preheated oven on the centre shelf for 45 mins. When cooked, removed the foil and arrange the fish, potatoes, mushrooms and juices on a heated serving plate. Garnish with slices of egg and sprigs of parsley.

HERRING

Herring is available in several forms. Matjes herrings are the young fish that have not yet grown a roe. The flesh is very perishable and they are therefore usually salted or pickled.

Green herrings are the mature fish that are caught shortly before they spawn. Fresh, unprocessed herring is available at the fishmonger. Smoked herring is called buckling and kipper. Herring salted at sea or on land is called salt herring and must be soaked before use.

Herring is very rich in protein and fat. The food on which the herring lives is of great importance. It is the plankton, tiny living organisms floating in the water, and the meat of small crayfish that give the flesh flavour and nutrients. In poor waters the herring remains lean and tasteless.

Grilled herring Maître d'Hôtel.

GRILLED HERRING MAÎTRE D'HÔTEL

Preparation time: 55 mins.
About 480 calories/2009 joules
Accompaniment: fried potatoes

Metric/Imperial	American
60g/2½ oz butter	¼ cup butter
1x15ml/1 tsp each chopped parsley and chives	1 tsp each chopped parsley and chives
1x15ml/1 tbs each chervil, tarragon, and dill	1 tbs each chervil, tarragon, and dill
1 shallot	1 shallot
salt, white pepper	salt, white pepper
4 fresh herrings, each 200g/7 oz	4 fresh herrings, each 7 oz
575ml/1 pint salted water	2½ cups salted water
40g/1½ oz flour	3 tbs flour
ice cubes	ice cubes
parsley for garnish	parsley for garnish

The herb butter in this recipe is called maître d'hôtel butter in international cuisine. Everything prepared with it may carry this name.

For the herb butter, put the butter and finely chopped herbs in a bowl. Add a grated shallot, salt, and pepper. Beat very well with a fork. Rinse a piece of greaseproof paper in cold water and place the butter on it. Shape into a roll about 4cm/1½ in thick and wrap in the paper. Place in the deep freezer or icemaking compartment of the refrigerator for 20 mins.

Gut the herrings, wash and pat dry. Place in a saucepan of boiling, salted water and poach for 5 mins. Remove and drain the fish. Roll in flour and place under a preheated grill for 4 mins. each side. Cut the butter into 2½cm/1 in thick slices. Arrange on a dish filled with ice cubes. Place the herrings on a preheated serving plate, and garnish with sprigs of parsley.

Herring Dieppe style is one of the special delights on offer in the little French seaport.

HERRING DIEPPE STYLE

Preparation time: 2 hrs. soaking, then 55 mins.
About 900 calories/3767 joules

Metric/Imperial	American
4 salt herrings, each 200g/7 oz gutted	4 salt herrings, each 7 oz, gutted
1¼kg/2½ lbs fresh mussels	2½ lbs fresh mussels
100g/4 oz frozen prawns	¼ lb frozen shrimps
250ml/8 fl oz water	1 cup water
For the fish liquor:	
375ml/12 fl oz water	1½ cups water
250g/8 fl oz dry white wine	1 cup dry white wine
juice 1 lemon	juice 1 lemon
1 onion	1 onion
1 shallot	1 shallot
3 parsley stalks	3 parsley stalks
100g/4 oz button mushrooms	¼ cup mushrooms
salt, white pepper	salt, white pepper
For the sauce:	
3 egg yolks	3 egg yolks
100g/4 oz butter	¼ lb butter
125ml/4 fl oz fish liquor	½ cup fish liquor
salt, white pepper	salt, white pepper
For the garnish:	
parsley	parsley
1 lemon	1 lemon

Wash the salt herrings inside and out. Place in a bowl, cover with cold water, and leave to soak for 2 hrs.

Scrub the mussels well under cold water. Defrost the shrimps. Bring the water to the boil and cook the mussels for about 10 mins. until they open up. Take out, remove the flesh from the shells, and cut off the beards with a sharp knife.

For the liquor, boil the water, white wine, lemon juice, onion cut in quarters, chopped shallot, and parsley stalks for 10 mins. Pour through a sieve into another saucepan. Add the drained herrings and mussels. Poach gently for 10 mins. Take out the herrings with a draining spoon and arrange on a heated serving plate. Surround with the drained mussels.

Slice the mushrooms thinly. Add to the fish liquor, bring to the boil, and cook for 5 mins. Then add the prawns and simmer for 5 mins. Do not boil. Remove the mushrooms and prawns with a draining spoon and arrange around the fish. Season lightly with salt and pepper.

For the sauce, mix the egg yolks with 1x15ml/1 tbs of the fish liquor. Beat until creamy over a pan of simmering water. Melt the butter and add to the egg yolks teaspoon by teaspoon. Then stir into 125ml/4 fl oz/½ cup of the fish liquor. Season with salt and pepper. Pour the sauce over the fish, and garnish with slices of lemon and sprigs of parsley.

BISMARCK HERRING

Preparation time: 5 mins.
About 49 calories/205 joules
Accompaniments: potatoes cooked in their skins and
peeled and a mixture of bacon and onions

Metric/Imperial	American
6 fillets of salt herring	6 fillets of salt herring
2 onions	2 onions
250ml/8 fl oz vinegar	1 cup vinegar
1 small bay leaf	1 small bay leaf
6–8 peppercorns	6–8 peppercorns
6–8 mustard seeds	6–8 mustard seeds

This dish was named after Otto, Count of Bismarck, the 19th-century German statesman, who was also a great gourmet.

Soak the salt herring fillets in cold water for at least 4 hrs. Drain and place in a deep bowl. Cover with the onions, cut in rings. Make a marinade of the vinegar, bay leaf, peppercorns, and mustard seeds. Pour over the fish and leave for at least 24 hrs. (48 hrs. would be better).

Another way to prepare this dish is to replace the vinegar with a generous cup of soured cream and 2x15ml/2 tbs lemon juice. Leave the herring fillets in this marinade for 48 hrs.

NORTH GERMAN HERRING PIE

Preparation time: 1 hr.
About 560 calories/2344 joules

Metric/Imperial	American
5 salt herrings, each 150g/5 oz	5 salt herrings, each 5 oz
375ml/12 fl oz milk	1½ cups milk
500g/1 lb cooked potatoes	1 lb cooked potatoes
butter for greasing	butter for greasing
60g/2½ oz butter	5 tbs butter
4 egg yolks	4 egg yolks
salt, black pepper	salt, black pepper
grated nutmeg	grated nutmeg
2 onions	2 onions
4 egg whites	4 egg whites
2x15ml/2 tbs dried breadcrumbs	2 tbs dried breadcrumbs
3x15ml/3 tbs cheese, grated	3 tbs cheese, grated
20g/¾ oz butter	1½ tbs butter

Served with vegetables or a salad, this herring pie brings variation to the menu. It can be prepared well in advance and stored in the refrigerator until 1 hr. before the meal, when it should be placed in the oven.
Preheat oven to 220°C/425°F/Gas 7. Gut the herrings and remove the bones. Cut off head, tail, and fins. Place in a bowl and leave to soak in milk for 10 mins. Mash the potatoes.

In a bowl beat 1½ oz/3 tbs butter with the egg yolks until frothy. Stir in the seasonings and mashed potatoes. Chop the onions and soften in the remaining butter until golden. Add to the potatoes. Drain and pat dry the fish. Cut in small pieces and stir into the potato mixture. Whip the egg whites until stiff and fold in. Pour into a greased, ovenproof pie dish. Sprinkle with breadcrumbs and grated cheese, and dot with butter. Place in the preheated oven for 1½ hrs.

TIP
Always gut fish carefully. Remove the black membranes of the inside as they make the fish taste bitter. Trim the back and tail fins.

North German herring pie.

MARINADED HERRING

Preparation time: 40 mins.
About 485 calories/2030 joules
Accompaniments: fried or jacket potatoes, or brown bread

Metric/Imperial	American
8 salt herrings, each 200g/7 oz	8 salt herrings, each 7 oz
3 onions	3 onions
1 pickled gherkin	1 pickled gherkin
few sprigs dill	few sprigs dill
1x15ml/1 tbs capers	1 tbs capers
For the marinade:	
125ml/4 fl oz white wine vinegar	½ cup white vinegar
125ml/4 fl oz water	½ cup water
2 bay leaves	2 bay leaves
10 peppercorns	10 peppercorns
3 cloves	3 cloves
1x15ml/1 tbs sugar	1 tbs sugar
2 sprigs parsley	2 sprigs parsley

If available, use the roe as well. Wash herrings and soak overnight in cold water to get rid of excess salt. Skin and remove heads, tails, and fins. Rinse and pat dry.

Slice the onions and gherkin. Layer the herring fillets, onions, gherkin, dill, and capers in a large bowl, glass jar, or deep ceramic dish. For the marinade, bring to the boil the vinegar, water, bay leaves, cloves, peppercorns, and sugar. Leave to cool. When cold, pour over the fish. Cover and leave for at least 24 hrs. Drain the herring fillets and arrange on a serving plate. Garnish with parsley.

Marinaded herring. ➤

CRISPY HERRING

Strömmings-Lada

Preparation time: 45 mins.
About 350 calories/1465 joules
Accompaniments: buttered potatoes tossed in parsley and mixed salad

Metric/Imperial	American
8 fresh herrings, each 150g/5 oz	8 fresh herrings, each 5 oz
juice 1 lemon	juice 1 lemon
margarine for greasing	margarine for greasing
salt	salt
25g/1 oz dried breadcrumbs	2 tbs dried breadcrumbs
25g/1 oz Parmesan cheese, grated	2 tbs Parmesan cheese, grated
50g/2 oz butter	4 tbs butter

Preheat oven to 220°C/425°F/Gas 7. Gut the herrings and carefully remove the fillets from the bones. Rinse and pat dry. Sprinkle with lemon juice and leave for 10 mins. Grease an ovenproof casserole, place herrings inside and sprinkle with salt. Cover with breadcrumbs and Parmesan cheese. Melt the butter and pour over the fish. Place in the preheated oven for 20 mins.

Strömmings-Lada is a tasty dish from the excellent cuisine of Sweden.

To prepare fried herring: first, spread mustard on the insides, then fold up and wrap evenly round with bacon.

FRIED HERRING

Preparation time: 45 mins.
About 925 calories/4123 joules

Metric/Imperial	American
8 fresh herrings	8 fresh herrings
juice 1 lemon	juice 1 lemon
salt	salt
4x15ml/4 tbs mustard	4 tbs mustard
200g/7 oz streaky bacon	7 oz fatty bacon slices
scant 125ml/4 fl oz olive oil	scant ½ cup olive oil
For the garnish:	
few lettuce leaves	few lettuce leaves
½ lemon	½ lemon
parsley	parsley

Scale the herrings, gut, wash, cut off heads, tails, and fins, and remove the bones. Sprinkle with lemon juice and a little salt. Open the herrings and cover the insides with mustard. Fold up again and wrap the bacon slices evenly round each fish. Fry in hot oil for about 10 min. each side until crisp. Arrange the lettuce leaves on a serving dish, place the herrings on top and garnish with lemon wedges and sprigs of parsley.

TIP
To remove the bones of herring, cut open the belly and open up the fish like a book. With your thumb, press along the backbone. Carefully pull the bones out of the flesh.

BAKED HERRING

Sillgratin

Preparation time: 1 hr.
About 535 calories/2239 joules

Metric/Imperial	American
4 fresh herrings, each 175g/6 oz	4 fresh herrings, each 6 oz
4 onions	4 onions
500g/1 lb potatoes	1 lb potatoes
75g/3 oz butter	6 tbs butter
white pepper, salt	white pepper, salt
3x15ml/3 tbs dried breadcrumbs	3 tbs dried breadcrumbs

Preheat oven to 240°C/450°F/gas 8. Gut the herrings and rinse inside and out under cold water. Pat dry. With a sharp knife, separate the fillets along the backbone on both sides. Cut each fillet into 3 long strips. Slice the onions and potatoes. Spread an ovenproof dish thickly with half the butter. Put a layer of potatoes on the bottom, then alternate layers of fish, onions, and potatoes. Finish with a layer of onions. Season each layer with salt and pepper as you go along. Sprinkle with breadcrumbs and dot with the remaining butter. Place in the preheated oven on the bottom shelf for 35 mins. If the breadcrumbs brown too quickly, cover the dish with foil.

EGYPTIAN HERRING

Preparation time: 1 hr. 10 mins.
About 905 calories/3788 joules

Metric/Imperial

8 fresh herrings,
   each 200g/7 oz
juice 1 lemon
2 onions
8 tomatoes
few sprigs parsley
salt
25g/1 oz flour
freshly ground black
   pepper
8x15ml/8 tbs oil
pinch each thyme,
   powdered garlic,
   and sugar
parsley for garnish

American

8 fresh herrings,
   each 7 oz
juice 1 lemon
2 onions
8 tomatoes
few sprigs parsley
salt
2 tbs flour
freshly ground black
   pepper
8 tbs oil
pinch each thyme,
   powdered garlic,
   and sugar
parsley for garnish

Scale the herrings under running water and gut. Cut off heads and tails. Rinse and sprinkle inside and out with lemon juice. Leave for 15 mins.

Chop onions finely. Skin, seed, and slice the tomatoes. Chop the parsley. Pat dry the herrings, season with salt, and roll in flour. Make sure there is flour in the insides, too. Heat the oil in a large frying pan. Add the fish and spoon some oil over them. Fry for 10 mins. each side until cooked. Season with pepper. Arrange on a heated serving plate and keep warm.

Add the chopped onions to the frying pan and fry until golden. Add the tomatoes and parsley and cook on a high heat for 5 mins. Season with salt, thyme, garlic, and sugar. Spread over the herrings and garnish with parsley.

Egyptian herring.

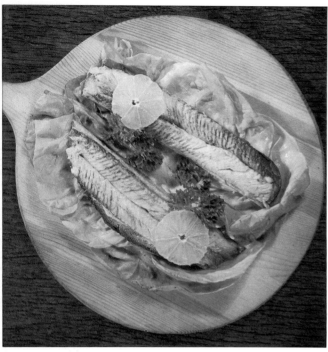

Simple but very good: Buckling on brown bread with parsley.

BUCKLING ON SCRAMBLED EGG

Preparation time: 35 mins.
361 calories/1511 joules

Metric/Imperial	American
2 bucklings	2 bucklings
4 eggs	4 eggs
4x15ml/4 tbs cream	4 tbs cream
salt, pepper	salt, pepper
few sprigs chives	few sprigs chives
40g/1½ oz butter	3 tbs butter

Make a cut on the back of the bucklings, pull off the skin and lift the fillets cleanly off the bones. Cut the flesh into bite-sized pieces. Mix the eggs with the cream. Season very lightly with salt and pepper as the buckling itself is quite salty. Snip the chives finely and add to the egg and cream mixture. Melt the butter in a frying pan and lightly fry the buckling pieces. Pour the egg mixture over and cook gently. Stir until scrambled and serve.

BUCKLING ON BROWN BREAD

Preparation time: 40 mins.
About 299 calories/1251 joules

Metric/Imperial	American
1 small round lettuce	1 small round lettuce
4 bucklings	4 bucklings
4 large slices brown or rye bread	4 large slices brown or rye bread
25g/1 oz butter	2 tbs butter
1 lemon	1 lemon
parsley	parsley

Wash the lettuce and pat dry. Make a cut on the back of the bucklings and pull off the skin. Lift the fillets off the bones with a knife. Butter the bread and cut in half. Arrange two halves on each plate, cover with lettuce leaves, and place the fillets on top. Garnish with peeled and sliced lemon and chopped parsley.

BUCKLING POTATOES

Preparation time: 35 mins.
356 calories/1490 joules

Metric/Imperial	American
2 bucklings	2 bucklings
750g/1½ lbs lightly cooked potatoes	1½ lbs lightly cooked potatoes
salt	salt
60g/2½ oz margarine	5 tbs margarine

Skin the bucklings and remove the bones. Cut into bite-sized pieces. Slice the potatoes and season with salt. Melt margarine in a frying pan and fry the sliced potatoes for 10 mins. Stir occasionally. Add the buckling pieces and continue frying for a further 5–10 mins. Serve hot.

NOTE:
You could layer the potatoes and fish in an ovenproof dish, pour over 2 beaten egg, and bake in the oven as an alternative.

MATJES

Every year, around the middle of May, Holland's fishermen compete in a tough race. And everywhere in the country people try to predict from which town the winner will come. The reason for the excitement: Matjes herring. From the middle of May until the beginning of June, it is caught in the northern North Sea, on the northern shores of Ireland, and on the east coast of Scotland.

When the first fishermen run into their home harbour with their catch, the race is over. The matjes, however, is really only a very ordinary herring. The only peculiarity is indicated by its name: Matjes—which means virgin herring. The fish is not yet mature, but it is just at that stage when it is most tender and succulent. However, it also perishes easily, and so it is salted straight away. Sometimes this is overdone and the fish's delicious taste is reduced.

A simple way to serve matjes, if it is not too salty, is as follows: do not soak, just gut. Dry carefully, cut into fillets, garnish with thin onion rings, and serve with butter and new potatoes.

Matjes fillets with juniper berries.

MATJES FILLETS WITH JUNIPER BERRIES

Preparation time before marinading: 45 mins.
About 465 calories/1946 joules

Metric/Imperial	American
8 matjes fillets, each 25g/1 oz	8 matjes fillets each 1 oz
250ml/8 fl oz milk	1 cup milk
3 onions	3 onions
2 cooking apples	2 cooking apples
3 small pickled gherkins	3 small pickled gherkins
1x5 ml/1 tsp juniper berries	1 tsp juniper berries
250ml/8 fl oz soured cream	1 cup sour cream
3x15ml/3 tbs mayonnaise	3 tbs mayonnaise
juice 1 lemon	juice 1 lemon
2x15ml/2 tbs oil	2 tbs oil
salt, white pepper	salt, white pepper
1 pinch of sugar	1 pinch of sugar
parsley and dill, to taste	parsley and dill

Soak the matjes fillets in milk for 1 hr. Take out, pat dry, and cut in bite-sized pieces. Slice the onions, and peel, core, and slice the apples. Layer with the matjes fillets and sliced pickled gherkins in a glazed earthenware dish. Sprinkle over the juniper berries. Mix the soured cream with the mayonnaise, lemon juice, and oil. Season with salt, pepper, sugar, and chopped parsley and dill. Pour over the fish. Cover and leave to marinade for at least 3–4 hours in the refrigerator.

Fried matjes kebabs.

FRIED MATJES KEBABS

Preparation time: 55 mins.
About 510 calories/2135 joules
Accompaniments: green salad and boiled potatoes or rice

Metric/Imperial	American
½ cucumber	½ cucumber
3 tomatoes	3 tomatoes
125g/4 oz button mushrooms	4 oz mushrooms
4 matjes fillets, each 25g/1 oz	4 matjes fillets, each 1 oz
3 thick slices streaky bacon	3 thick slices fatty bacon
125g/4 oz Gouda cheese	¼ lb Gouda cheese
1 onion	1 onion
125ml/4 fl oz water, salt	½ cup water, salt
freshly ground black pepper	freshly ground black pepper
Worcester sauce	Worcester sauce
25g/1 oz flour	2 tbs flour
1 egg	1 egg
2x15ml/2 tbs dried breadcrumbs	2 tbs dried breadcrumbs
2x15ml/2 tbs Emmenthal cheese, grated	2 tbs Swiss cheese, grated
1x5ml/1 tsp paprika	1 tsp paprika
4x15ml/4 tbs oil	4 tbs oil
parsley for garnish	parsley for garnish

Peel and seed the cucumber. Skin, quarter, and seed the tomatoes. Prepare the mushrooms. Cut the matjes fillets, cucumber, bacon, and Gouda cheese in 5½cm/2 in cubes. Quarter the onion. Bring a pan of salted water to the boil and cook the cucumber and onion pieces for 5 mins. Drain and cool. Thread all the ingredients on to 8 kebab sticks or skewers and season with pepper and Worcester sauce.

Put the flour on a plate, beat the egg on a second plate, and mix the breadcrumbs, grated cheese, and paprika on a third. Roll the kebebs first in flour, then in egg, and last in the breadcrumb mixture.

Heat the oil in frying pan and fry the kebabs gently for 5 mins. on all sides. Arrange on a heated serving plate with the chopped parsley, and serve immediately.

MATJES FILLETS WITH PRAWNS

Preparation time: 25 mins.
About 415 calories/1737 joules

Metric/Imperial	American
4 matjes fillets (250ml/8 fl oz milk, if necessary)	4 matjes fillets (1 cup milk, if necessary)
For the sauce:	
250ml/8 fl oz cream	1 cup cream
150g/5 oz plain yogurt	5 oz plain yogurt
juice 1 lemon	juice 1 lemon
sugar, white pepper	sugar, white pepper
1 small onion	1 small onion
1 hardboiled egg	1 hardboiled egg
1x15ml/1 tbs fresh or 1 tsp dried dill	1 tbs fresh or 1 tsp dried dill
150g/5 oz prawns	5 oz shrimps
For the garnish:	
1 pickled gherkin	1 pickled gherkin
1 hardboiled egg	1 hardboiled egg

Wash the matjes fillets. (If they are very salty, soak them in milk for 10 mins.) Pat dry and arrange on a serving dish.

For the sauce, beat the cream and yogurt in a bowl until very frothy. Season well with lemon juice, sugar, and pepper. Chop the onion, egg, and dill finely. Mix with the cream and yogurt. Prepare the prawns, reserve a few for garnish, and fold gently into the sauce. Pour over the matjes fillets.

Sprinkle over the remaining prawns, and garnish with sliced gherkin and slices of hardboiled egg.

MACKEREL

It is because of its torpedo-shaped body that the mackerel can reach those remarkable speeds with which it cruises through the Mediterranean, the Atlantic Ocean, the North Sea, and the Baltic.

The green or blue mackerel has very small scales, black stripes across the back, and a pearly white belly. It can reach a length of up to 60cm/2 ft, but it is usually only about 30cm/1 ft long when it reaches the fishmonger's slab. Mackerel live in large shoals and only approach the coast during spawning time in June and July. Then they retreat back into the ocean. From October until April they regain their high-quality, firm and tasty flesh which then is also quite oily. 100g/4 oz of mackerel flesh contains about 12% oil and about 19% protein and traces of carbohydrates. That is about 195 calories.

Mackerel can be prepared in a number of ways: whether it is poached, smoked, salted, marinaded in oil, or served with fine sauces, the mackerel is always tasty. It is especially popular because it contains only comparatively few bones.

Whether poached, smoked, salted, or served with fine sauces, mackerel always tastes good.

Soured cream makes Mackerel Zoppot style especially tasty.

MACKEREL ZOPPOT STYLE

Preparation time: 1 hr. 15 mins.
About 330 calories/1381 joules

Metric/Imperial	American
4 mackerel, each 200g/7 oz	**4 mackerel, each 7 oz**
juice 1 lemon	**juice 1 lemon**
2 onions	**2 onions**
250g/8 oz tomatoes	**½ lb tomatoes**
100g/4 oz button mush-rooms, sliced thinly	**4 oz mushrooms, sliced thinly**
25g/1 oz margarine	**2 tbs margarine**
salt, white pepper	**salt, white pepper**
1 pinch dried thyme	**1 pinch dried thyme**
125ml/4 fl oz soured cream	**½ cup sour cream**

Gut the mackerel and rinse inside and out under cold water. Pat dry and sprinkle inside and out with lemon juice. Cover and leave for 10 mins. Meanwhile, dice the onions, and skin, seed, and chop the tomatoes roughly. Melt the margarine in a large frying pan and soften the onion until golden. Stir in the tomatoes and seasoning. Add the mushrooms and cook for 10 mins. Place the mackerel on top of the vegetables, cover, and cook gently for 20 mins. Arrange on a heated serving dish. Beat the soured cream and pour over the mackerel. Serve immediately.

Mackerel Alsace style: served with sauerkraut and bacon.

MACKEREL ON PEPPERS

Preparation time: 1 hr. 10 mins.
About 430 calories/1800 joules

Metric/Imperial	American
4 mackerel, each 200g/7 oz	4 mackerel, each 7 oz
juice 1 lemon	juice 1 lemon
4 onions	4 onions
4 red or green sweet peppers	4 red or green sweet peppers
8 tomatoes	8 tomatoes
5x15ml/5 tbs oil	5 tbs oil
salt, black pepper	salt, black pepper
paprika	paprika
1 clove garlic	1 clove garlic
2x15ml/2 tbs parsley, chopped	2 tbs parsley, chopped
125ml/4 fl oz white wine	½ cup white wine

Preheat oven to 200°C/400°F/Gas 6. Gut the mackerel, wash inside and out, and pat dry. Cut in half lengthwise and remove the backbones. Sprinkle with lemon juice.

Dice the onions, seed the peppers, and cut in narrow strips. Skin, seed, and chop the tomatoes roughly. Heat the oil in an ovenproof casserole and soften the onions for 5 mins. until golden. Add the peppers, tomatoes, and seasonings. Cook gently for 15 mins.

Chop the garlic finely and sprinkle over the vegetables. Place the mackerel fillets on top, sprinkle with chopped parsley, and pour over the white wine. Cover and place in the preheated oven on the centre shelf for 20 mins.

BAKED MACKEREL

Preparation time: 40 mins.
About 425 calories/1779 joules
Accompaniments: buttered potatoes and young peas

Metric/Imperial	American
4 mackerel, each 200g/7 oz	4 mackerel, each 7 oz
salt, white pepper	salt, white pepper
4x15ml/4 tbs mustard	4 tbs mustard
few sprigs each parsley and dill	few sprigs each parsley and dill
4 bay leaves	4 bay leaves
margarine for greasing	margarine for greasing
250ml/8 fl oz cream	1 cup cream

Preheat oven to 200°C/400°F/Gas 6. Gut the mackerel, rinse inside and out, and pat dry. Make a few slashes across the back. Season inside and out with salt and pepper and spread with mustard.

Chop the parsley and dill finely. Stuff each fish with a bay leaf, parsley, and dill. Fasten with wooden cocktail sticks. Place the mackerel in a greased, ovenproof dish and pour the cream over. Place in the preheated oven on the centre shelf for 15 mins.

NOTE:
You could also deep fry the mackerel. Just roll in some flour after seasoning. Serve with a tomato sauce.

MACKEREL ALSAÇE STYLE

Preparation time: 65 mins.
About 670 calories/2804 joules

Metric/Imperial	American
1 onion, finely chopped	1 onion, finely chopped
75g/3 oz margarine	⅓ cup margarine
750g/1½ lbs sauerkraut	1½ lbs sauerkraut
125ml/4 fl oz white wine	½ cup white wine
4 mackerel, each 200g/7 oz	4 mackerel, each 7 oz
juice 1 lemon	juice 1 lemon
salt, black pepper	salt, black pepper
4x15ml/4 tbs flour	4 tbs flour
6 slices streaky bacon	6 slices fatty bacon
For the garnish:	
parsley	parsley
1 lemon, sliced	1 lemon, sliced

Melt ⅓ margarine in a saucepan and cook the chopped onion for 1 min. until golden. Add the sauerkraut and wine, cover, and cook for 30 mins.

In the meantime, gut the mackerel and rinse inside and out under cold water. Dry well and sprinkle with lemon juice. Season, and roll in flour. Melt ½ margarine in a frying pan and fry the mackerel for 5 mins. each side. Keep warm.

Melt the remaining margarine and fry the bacon for 3 mins. Arrange the sauerkraut on a heated oval serving dish. Place first the bacon and then the mackerel on top. Garnish with lemon slices and parsley.

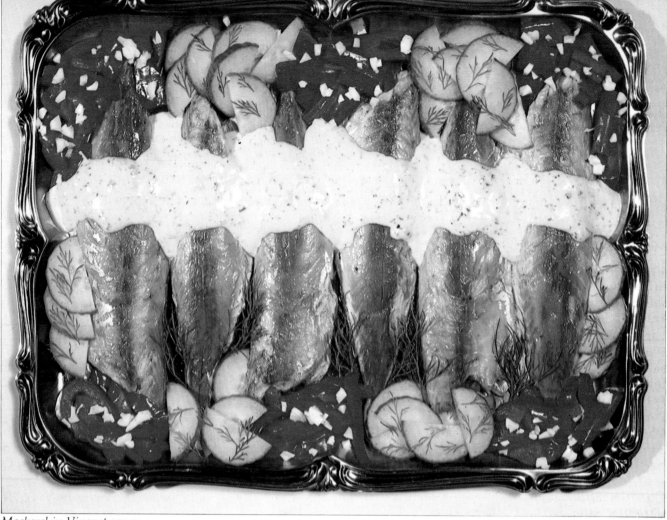

Mackerel in Vincent sauce.

MACKEREL IN VINCENT SAUCE

Preparation time: 50 mins.
About 815 calories/3411 joules
Accompaniments: fresh crusty bread or jacket potatoes

Metric/Imperial	American
4 mackerel, each 200g/7 oz	4 mackerel, each 7 oz
juice 1 lemon	juice 1 lemon
1 carrot, 1 leek, 1 stick celery	1 carrot, 1 leek, 1 stick celery
1 onion	1 onion
1 small bay leaf	1 small bay leaf
1x5ml/1 tsp mustard seeds	1 tsp mustard seeds
2 cloves	2 cloves
2 juniper berries	2 juniper berries
1 litre/1¾ pints salted water	4½ cups salted water
For the sauce:	
few sprigs each parsley and chives	few sprigs each parsley and chives
2 hardboiled eggs	2 hardboiled eggs
250ml/8 fl oz mayonnaise	1 cup mayonnaise
1x15ml/1 tbs tarragon vinegar	1 tbs tarragon vinegar
Worcester sauce	Worcester sauce
For the garnish:	
1 jar pickled red peppers	1 jar pickled red peppers
1 cucumber	1 cucumber
few sprigs dill	few sprigs dill
salt, white pepper	salt, white pepper

Gut the mackerel, cut off heads, tails, and fins, and wash and pat dry. Sprinkle inside and out with lemon juice.

Roughly chop the carrot, leek, and celery. Cut the onion in quarters. Place vegetables and seasonings in a saucepan of salted water and bring to the boil. Add the mackerel and poach for 15 mins. Cool in the liquor.

For the sauce, chop the parsley and chives. Separate the yolks from the whites of eggs, and mash in a bowl. Chop the whites of egg. Stir the herbs and mayonnaise into the mashed yolks, and season with tarragon vinegar and Worcester sauce. Drain the cooled mackerel and pat dry. Carefully remove the fillets from the bones and skin. Arrange in the centre of a serving dish. Drain the pickled red peppers. Slice the cucumber. Chop the dill. Surround the mackerel fillets with strips of red pepper and cucumber slices. Season with salt and pepper. Sprinkle with dill and chopped egg whites. Either pour the sauce over the dish or serve separately.

GRILLED MACKEREL WITH HERB BUTTER

Preparation time: 1 hr.
About 450 calories/1883 joules
Accompaniments: green salad and potatoes tossed in butter and parsley

Metric/Imperial	American
4 mackerel, each 200g/7 oz	4 mackerel, each 7 oz
juice 1 lemon	juice 1 lemon
salt, white pepper	salt, white pepper
4x15ml/4 tbs oil	4 tbs oil
For the herb butter:	
50g/2 oz butter	4 tbs butter
salt, white pepper	salt, white pepper
few sprigs parsley	few sprigs parsley
1x15ml/1 tsp lemon juice	1 tsp lemon juice
For the garnish:	
4 lemon slices	4 lemon slices
2 tomatoes	2 tomatoes
parsley	parsley

Gut the mackerel and wash inside and out. Carefully remove the bones through a slit in the back. Open up like a book and place in a bowl. Sprinkle with lemon juice and season inside and out. Pour the oil over the fish, cover, and leave for 35 mins. in the refrigerator.

For the herb butter, mix the butter with salt, pepper, chopped parsley, and lemon juice. Shape into a roll, wrap in dampened greaseproof paper and chill in the refrigerator for 30 mins.

Place the mackerel on a grill rack and grill first on the skin side and then on the inside for 5 mins. each. Remove to a heated serving plate. Cut the butter in 4 slices and place, with the lemon slices, on top of the fish. Garnish with quarters of tomatoes and chopped parsley.

PERCH JOINVILLE

Preparation time: 40 mins.
About 430 calories/1796 joules
Accompaniments: peas and boiled potatoes, tossed in butter and parsley

Metric/Imperial	American
4 medium-sized perch	4 medium-sized perch
juice 1 lemon	juice 1 lemon
salt	salt
50g/2 oz butter	4 tbs butter
250g/8 oz button mushrooms	½ lb mushrooms
250g/8 oz prawns	½ lb shrimp
few sprigs parsley, chopped	few sprigs parsley, chopped
250ml/8 fl oz white wine	1 cup white wine
pepper	pepper
1 egg yolk	1 egg yolk
2x15ml/2 tbs cream	2 tbs cream

The perch is a freshwater fish of prey. It can reach a length of 35cm/14 in. and can weigh up to almost 2kg/4½ lbs. Its flesh is firm and white. Unfortunately, it is not available everywhere, but it is worth buying when you can.

Clean the fish, remove scales, and cut in fillets: i.e., lift the flesh off the bones from head to tail. Sprinkle with lemon juice and salt. Melt the butter and lightly fry the fillets. Slice the mushrooms, keeping a few for garnish, and add with half the prawns, half the chopped parsley, and the white wine to the pan. Cook for about 10 mins. Remove the fish and arrange on a warmed serving plate. Season the liquor with salt and pepper, and add the remaining prawns, leaving a few for garnish. Mix the egg yolk with the cream, pour in and cook gently until thickened. Pour the sauce over the fillets and garnish with parsley and a few mushrooms and prawns.

Grilled mackerel, garnished with herb butter.

Flamed with brandy, the fennel perch becomes especially aromatic.

FENNEL PERCH

Preparation time: 55 mins.
About 520 calories/2176 joules

Metric/Imperial	American
1 perch, about 1kg/2¼ lbs	1 perch, 2¼ lbs
juice 1 lemon	juice 1 lemon
1 large head of fennel	1 large head of fennel
1¼ml/¼ tsp dried sage	¼ tsp dried sage
salt	salt
2x15ml/2 tbs flour	2 tbs flour
50g/2 oz butter	4 tbs butter
1 lemon	1 lemon
few sprigs parsley	few sprigs parsley
3x15ml/3 tbs brandy	3 tbs brandy

Rinse the perch, gut, and remove scales. Rinse again and pat dry. Sprinkle inside and out evenly with lemon juice. Trim the fennel, remove outer leaves but leave a few pale green stalks. Quarter and dice finely. Mix 4x15ml/4 tbs of fennel with sage and salt. Stuff into the fish and fasten with a wooden cocktail stick. Sprinkle with salt and roll in flour. Melt the butter in a large frying pan. Fry the fish quickly for 3 mins. on each side until browned, and continue frying gently for a further 10 mins. each side. Place the remaining diced fennel on to a serving plate and arrange the fish on top. Pour over the cooking juices. Garnish with lemon slices and parsley. Pour the brandy over and set alight. Serve while still flaming.

PERCH FILLETS ON SAFFRON RICE

Preparation time: 1 hr. 20 mins.
About 595 calories/2491 joules
Accompaniments: mixed or green salad

Metric/Imperial	American
4 small perch	4 small perch
white pepper	white pepper
juice 1 lemon	juice 1 lemon
For the rice:	
1 onion	1 onion
40g/1½ oz butter	3 tbs butter
125g/4 oz long grain rice	½ cup long grain rice
375ml/12 fl oz hot stock	1½ cups hot stock
salt	salt
1 pinch of saffron	1 pinch of saffron
2 large tomatoes	2 large tomatoes
In addition:	
salt	salt
25g/1 oz flour	2 tbs flour
2 eggs	2 eggs
2½ml/½ tsp dried sage, crumbled	½ tsp dried sage, crumbled
75g/3 oz butter or margarine	⅓ cup butter or margarine
few sprigs chives for garnish	few sprigs chives for garnish

Gut the perch, scale, and cut in fillets. Rinse under cold water and pat dry. Sprinkle with pepper and lemon juice, cover, and leave for 1 hr.

In the meantime, chop the onion finely. Melt the butter in an ovenproof casserole and fry the onion for 2 mins. until transparent. Wash the rice well in a sieve under cold water. Drain and add to the onion. Stirring constantly, fry for 5 mins. Pour in the hot stock, stir, and season with salt and saffron. Cover, and cook the rice for 20 mins. until all the liquid has evaporated. Skin, seed and dice the tomatoes. Spread them over the rice 10 mins. before the end of the cooking time.

Drain the fillets of perch, season with salt, and roll in flour. Beat the eggs on a plate and mix with the sage. Melt the butter or margarine in a frying pan. Dip the fillets in the egg mixture and fry for 4 mins. each side. Arrange on the cooked rice. Garnish with snipped chives, and serve immediately in the casserole.

PIKE

Pike is a ferocious fish of prey. It usually lives in ponds and devours almost any other living fish in them. The protein of its prey gives the pike its flavour. It can also be found, however, in many lakes and rivers from middle Europe to the far north; and there it even eats fish of its own kind.

It is said that there are pike weighing over 50kg/110 lbs in Siberian rivers. Even in middle Europe, female pike of 15kg/33 lbs and a respectable length of 1m/3 ft have been caught. Male pike are usually smaller. Fat pike of either sex, however, are not very nice. It is best to eat young pike: in their second year, they have the most delicate and tastiest flesh and weigh up to 2kg/4½ lbs. One-year-old pike are smaller and are usually fried. Otherwise, pike—if not filleted—is best poached, steamed, or boiled, although sometimes it is prepared 'blue', like trout or carp.

For many fish gourmets, the pike is the king of all freshwater fish. Its only disadvantage is that it has many bones: you need patience and a steady hand to enjoy eating pike!

Pike St. Germain.

PIKE ST. GERMAIN

Preparation time: 55 mins.
About 425 calories/1779 joules

Metric/Imperial	American
4 fillets of pike, each 250g/8 oz	4 fillets of pike, each ½ lb
2x15ml/2 tbs lemon juice	2 tbs lemon juice
For the Béarnaise sauce:	
2 shallots	2 shallots
3x15ml/3 tbs tarragon vinegar	3 tbs tarragon vinegar
3 peppercorns	3 peppercorns
2x5ml/2 tsp meat extract	2 tsp meat extract
3 egg yolks	3 egg yolks
1x15ml/1 tbs warm water	1 tbs warm water
100g/4 oz butter	½ cup butter
2½ml/½ tsp salt, cayenne pepper	½ tsp salt, cayenne pepper
1x15ml/1 tbs fresh tarragon, chopped or 1x5ml/1 tsp dried chervil	1 tbs fresh tarragon, chopped or 1 tsp dried chervil
4 tomatoes	4 tomatoes
salt, white pepper	salt, white pepper
25g/1 oz flour	2 tbs flour
25g/1 oz butter	2 tbs butter

For the garnish:

few sprigs parsley	few sprigs parsley
1 lemon	1 lemon

Wash the fillets of pike and pat dry. Sprinkle with lemon juice.

For the sauce, chop the shallots finely. Bring to the boil with the tarragon vinegar, peppercorns, and meat extract. The shallots must still be transparent. Strain. Mix the egg yolks with warm water. Whisk until creamy over a pan of simmering water. Melt the butter, and gradually add to the egg yolks 1 tsp at a time. Add the shallot liquor, salt, pepper, and chopped herbs, stirring continuously. Cut off the stalk ends of the tomatoes. Make a cross cut into the top and sprinkle with salt and pepper.

Pat the fillets of pike dry again, season, and roll in flour. Melt the butter and trickle over the fish. Place the fillets under a preheated grill and lay the tomatoes beside them. Grill for 4 mins. each side. Arrange the fish and tomatoes on a serving plate. Pour a little sauce over and garnish with lemon wedges and sprigs of parsley. Serve the remaining sauce separately.

Pike in white wine.

PIKE IN WHITE WINE

Preparation time: 30 mins.
About 360 calories/1507 joules

Metric/Imperial

2 young pike, each
    500g/1 lb
juice 1 lemon
salt, white pepper
1 onion
2 cloves garlic
few sprigs parsley
8x15ml/8 tbs oil
250ml/8 fl oz white wine
juice ½ lemon
1 pinch of sugar
1x15ml/1 tbs cornflour

American

2 young pike, each
    1 lb
juice 1 lemon
salt, white pepper
1 onion
2 cloves garlic
few sprigs parsley
½ cup oil
1 cup white wine
juice ½ lemon
1 pinch of sugar
1 tbs cornstarch

Slit open the belly of the pike and gut. Rinse well inside and out. Drain and cut into 5½cm/2 in. pieces. Sprinkle with lemon juice, salt, and pepper. Cover and set aside.

Dice the onion finely and crush the garlic. Chop the parsley finely. Heat the oil in a large frying pan and fry the pieces of pike for 2 mins. Add the onion, garlic, and parsley and fry for a further 2 mins. Pour in the white wine and lemon juice and season with salt, pepper, and sugar. Cover and simmer gently for 10 mins.

Mix the cornflour with a little cold water and stir into the pan. Bring quickly to the boil. Arrange the pike on a large serving plate, pour over the sauce, and serve immediately.

PIKE POACHED IN BEER

Preparation time: 1 hr. 15 mins.
About 455 calories/1904 joules

Metric/Imperial	American
1 pike, about 1kg/2¼ lbs	1 pike, about 2¼ lbs
juice 1 lemon	juice 1 lemon
1 large leek	1 large leek
3 carrots	3 carrots
2 onions	2 onions
100g/4 oz celeriac	¼ lb celeriac
50g/2 oz butter	4 tbs butter
salt	salt
125ml/4 fl oz hot stock	½ cup hot stock
125ml/4 fl oz dark ale	½ cup dark beer
½ bay leaf	½ bay leaf
3 mustard seeds	3 mustard seeds
3 white peppercorns	3 white peppercorns
25g/1 oz flour	2 tbs flour
250ml/8 fl oz soured cream	1 cup sour cream
chives for garnish	chives for garnish

Scale the pike under running cold water. Gut and rinse well. Pat dry, sprinkle with lemon juice, and set aside.

Trim the leek, and cut in slices. Cut the carrots, onions, and celeriac into narrow strips. Melt the butter in a saucepan. Gently fry the vegetables for 5 mins., stirring occasionally. Season with salt and pour in the hot stock. Simmer for a further 5 mins., then add the dark ale, ½ bay leaf, and the spices. Bring to the boil. Insert the pike, cover, and poach very gently for 25 mins., until cooked. Carefully take out the fish with a draining spoon and arrange on a heated plate. Keep warm. Strain the sauce and return to the saucepan. Mix the flour with soured cream and stir into the sauce. Cook for 5 mins. and season to taste. Pour the sauce over the pike, and garnish with finely chopped chives.

TIP
The length of cooking time for pike depends on the age of the fish. You can be sure it is properly cooked when you can pull out the back fin quite easily.

STUFFED PIKE

Preparation time: 25 mins.
About 530 calories/2218 joules

Metric/Imperial	American
100g/4 oz streaky bacon	¼ lb fatty bacon
1 pike, about 1½kg/3½ lbs	1 pike, about 3½ lbs
4x15ml/4 tbs vinegar	4 tbs vinegar
For the stuffing:	
1 stale bread roll	1 stale bread roll
125ml/4 fl oz milk	½ cup milk
100g/4 oz streaky bacon	¼ lb fatty bacon
2 onions, finely chopped	2 onions, finely chopped
200g/7 oz button mushrooms	7 oz mushrooms
2 egg yolks	2 egg yolks
few sprigs parsley	few sprigs parsley
5 sprigs of fresh or 1 tsp dried dill	5 sprigs of fresh or 1 tsp dried dill
white pepper, salt	white pepper, salt
1x15ml/1 tbs oil for greasing	1 tbs oil for greasing
For the garnish:	
2 lemons	2 lemons
4 sprigs parsley	4 sprigs parsley
8 strips pickled red peppers	8 strips pickled red peppers

Preheat oven to 200°C/400°F/Gas 6. Cut the bacon in ¼-in strips. Place in the icemaking compartment of the refrigerator for 15 mins. Meanwhile, gut the pike, remove scales, and rinse inside and out. Pat dry and sprinkle with vinegar. Then lard the pike: using a larding needle, insert the strips of chilled bacon into the flesh of the back.

For the stuffing soak the bread roll in milk for 10 mins. Cut the bacon in ½cm/¼ in cubes. Fry gently in a frying pan until the fat runs. Add the finely chopped onions and fry until golden. Add the finely sliced mushrooms and cook for 3 mins., stirring occasionally. Mix all well with the squeezed bread roll and egg yolks in a bowl. Chop the parsley and dill finely and mix into the stuffing. Season well with salt and pepper. Stuff the pike with the mixture, fasten with a cocktail stick and sprinkle the outside with salt. Line a baking tray with foil, grease with oil, and place the fish on it. Put in the preheated oven on the centre shelf for 40 mins. Arrange the pike on a heated serving dish, and garnish with lemon slices, sprigs of parsley, and strips of pickled red peppers.

TIP
Ask your fishmonger to scale and gut the pike for you.

PIKE DUMPLINGS WITH MUSHROOMS

Preparation time: 1 hr. 25 mins.
About 1470 calories/6153 joules
Accompaniments: green salad and boiled rice. It looks
very pretty when served in a ring of rice.

Metric/Imperial	American
500g/1 lb fillets of pike, skinned	**1 lb fillets of pike, skinned**
200g/7 oz beef suet	**1 cup shredded suet**
250ml/8 fl oz milk	**1 cup milk**
50g/2 oz butter	**4 tbs butter**
125g/4 oz flour	**1 cup flour**
4 eggs	**4 eggs**
salt, white pepper	**salt, white pepper**
1x15ml/1 tbs mixed chopped herbs (parsley, tarragon, chervil)	**1 tbs mixed chopped herbs (parsley, tarragon, chervil)**
1 litre/1¾ pints water	**4½ cups water**
250g/8 oz button mushrooms	**½ lb mushrooms**
125ml/4 fl oz water	**½ cup water**
juice ½ lemon	**juice ½ lemon**
25g/1 oz butter	**2 tbs butter**
300g/10 oz tinned crayfish tails	**10 oz canned crayfish tails**
For the white wine sauce:	
25g/1 oz butter or margarine	**2 tbs butter or margarine**
25g/1 oz flour	**2 tbs flour**
125ml/4 fl oz fish dumpling liquor	**½ cup fish dumpling liquor**
125ml/4 fl oz mushroom liquor	**½ cup mushroom liquor**
250ml/8 fl oz white wine	**1 cup white wine**
salt, white pepper	**salt, white pepper**
juice ½ lemon	**juice ½ lemon**
For the Hollandaise sauce:	
100g/4 oz butter	**½ cup butter**
1 egg yolk	**1 egg yolk**
1x15ml/1 tbs water	**1 tbs water**
salt, white pepper	**salt, white pepper**
cayenne pepper	**cayenne pepper**
2½ml/½ tsp lemon juice	**½ tsp lemon juice**
For the garnish:	
8–10 puff pastry fleurons	**8–10 puff pastry fleurons**

Mince the fillets of pike and suet finely. Bring the milk and butter to the boil in a saucepan. Quickly beat in the flour all at once. Stir vigorously until the mixture draws away from the bottom of the pan. Add 2 eggs and leave to cool.

Mix the choux pastry with the minced fish and suet in a bowl. Add the 2 remaining eggs and season with salt and pepper. Rub the mixture through a sieve and stir well again. Mix one half of the mixture with the herbs.

In a large, shallow casserole, bring the water to the boil. Add salt. With the aid of a teaspoon, shape about 50 small dumplings from both fish mixtures. Slip into the water and poach gently for 15 mins.

Trim the mushrooms, and halve large ones. In a saucepan, bring the water with lemon juice and half the butter to the boil. Add salt. Cook the mushrooms for 5 mins. Reserve the liquor. Drain the crayfish tails and cut in half. Melt the remaining butter, and fry the crayfish tails for 5 mins.

Remove the dumplings with a draining spoon, drain, and leave covered on a heated plate. Keep the liquor.

For the white wine sauce, melt the butter or margarine in a saucepan. Add the flour and cook for a few mins. Then pour in the fish liquor and mushroom water and cook until reduced slightly. Add the white wine and season with salt, pepper, and lemon juice.

For the Hollandaise sauce, melt the butter, remove the foam that rises to the top, and cool. Mix the egg yolk with water and whisk over a bowl of hot water until thick and frothy. Remove from the heat, and very gradually add the melted butter. Season with salt, white pepper, cayenne pepper, and lemon juice. Remove the white wine sauce from the heat, and fold in the Hollandaise sauce. Lightly stir the dumplings into the sauce with the mushrooms and crayfish tails. Arrange in a shallow serving dish, surround with puff pastry fleurons, and serve hot.

Pike dumplings with mushrooms.

PIKE WITH HERBS AND BREADCRUMBS

Preparation time: 1 hr. 10 mins.
About 250 calories/1046 joules

Metric/Imperial	American
1 pike, about 1¼kg/2¾ lbs	1 pike, about 2¾ lbs
25g/1 oz butter	2 tbs butter
4 shallots or 2 onions	4 shallots or 2 onions
25g/1 oz anchovy fillets	1 oz anchovy fillets
salt, white pepper	salt, white pepper
125ml/4 fl oz dry white wine	½ cup dry white wine
few sprigs chervil	few sprigs chervil
2x15ml/2 tbs Emmenthal cheese, grated	2 tbs Swiss cheese, grated
1x15ml/1 tbs dried breadcrumbs	1 tbs dried breadcrumbs

Preheat oven to 200°C/400°F/Gas 6. Gut the pike, cut off head and tail. Wash and cut in half along the backbone. Remove backbone and small bones. Skin the fish and cut in 4 pieces.

Grease an ovenproof pie dish with a little butter. Chop the shallots or onions finely, and sprinkle over the dish. Place the fish on top, and cover with anchovy fillets. Melt remaining butter and pour over. Season well with salt and pepper. Pour in the white wine, cover the dish, and place in the preheated oven on the centre shelf for 30 mins.

Meanwhile, chop the chervil finely, and mix together the cheese and breadcrumbs. Remove the fish from the oven and sprinkle with first, the chopped chervil and then the breadcrumb mixture. Increase oven temperature to 240°C/475°F/Gas 9. Return the dish to the hot oven on the top shelf for 5 mins. to let the crumbs brown.

TIP
Pike with herbs and breadcrumbs tastes even better if it is flavoured not only with chervil, but also with the classic French herb mixture *Fines Herbes*, consisting of chervil, parsley, chives, and tarragon.

PLAICE

Plaice are usually fairly small flat fish. The main catch areas are the North Sea and the Baltic.

Some people consider the dark brown upper skin, with its bright orange spots, a delicacy when fried. The flesh is light and easily digestible. Fresh plaice are usually fried or are sometimes poached and served with mustard sauce. The average weight of a plaice is 250g/ 8 oz, so serve one per person.

PLAICE WITH HERBS

Preparation time: 40 mins.
About 580 calories/2428 joules

Metric/Imperial	American
4 plaice, cleaned and gutted	4 plaice, cleaned and gutted
juice 1 lemon	juice 1 lemon
salt, white pepper	salt, white pepper
4x15ml/4 tbs ground almonds	4 tbs ground almonds
75g/3 oz butter or margarine	⅓ cup butter or margarine
few sprigs each dill and parsley	few sprigs each dill and parsley
4 sprigs lemon balm	4 sprigs lemon balm
2 sprigs fresh tarragon	2 sprigs fresh tarragon
2 eggs	2 eggs
125ml/4 fl oz cream	½ cup cream
25g/1 oz butter	2 tbs butter

Preheat oven to 200°C/400°F/Gas 6. Carefully wash the plaice, and cut off fins and tails. Pat dry. Sprinkle both sides with lemon juice, cover and leave for 15 mins.

Season the fish on both sides. Roll in ground almonds, patting them on firmly. Reserve any left over. Melt the butter or margarine in a large frying pan and fry the plaice for 3 mins. each side. Remove and place in a shallow, greased ovenproof dish.

Chop the parsley, dill, lemon balm, and tarragon finely. Put the eggs and cream into a bowl, add the chopped herbs and salt, and mix well. Pour over the plaice. Sprinkle with remaining ground almonds and dot with butter. Place the dish in the preheated oven on the centre shelf for 15 mins.

Plaice with herbs.

Fillets of plaice Holmsland style are served on a bed of lettuce, prawns, pineapple, and tomatoes.

FILLETS OF PLAICE HOLMSLAND STYLE

Preparation time: 40 mins.
About 350 calories/1465 joules
Accompaniments: crusty French bread or potato crisps

Metric/Imperial	American
For the salad:	
1 round lettuce	1 round lettuce
100g/4 oz tinned pineapple slices	4 oz canned pineapple slices
2 tomatoes	2 tomatoes
100g/4 oz prawns	4 oz shrimps
3x15ml/3 tbs mayonnaise	3 tbs mayonnaise
1x15ml/1 tbs cream	1 tbs cream
1x15ml/1 tbs lemon juice	1 tbs lemon juice
1x5ml/1 tsp herb mustard	1 tsp herb mustard
8 fillets of plaice	8 fillets of plaice
salt, white pepper	salt, white pepper
40g/1½ oz flour	3 tbs flour
oil for deep frying	oil for deep frying
2 lemons for garnish	2 lemons for garnish

Holmsland is a district containing several small villages on the west coast of Denmark.

For the salad, shred the lettuce finely. Drain the pineapple slices and cut in cubes. Chop the tomatoes, and prepare the prawns. Mix all together in a large bowl. Mix the mayonnaise with the cream, lemon juice, and mustard and pour over the salad.

Season the fillets of plaice, and roll in flour. Heat the oil in a deep fat fryer to 180°C/350°F. Fry the fillets for 5 mins. until crispy and golden brown. Remove fish and drain on kitchen paper. Stir the salad once and arrange the plaice on top. Garnish with the lemons, cut in wedges.

PLAICE IN WHITE WINE

Preparation time: 35 mins.
About 310 calories/1297 joules

Metric/Imperial	American
4 plaice, each 250g/8 oz, cleaned and gutted	4 plaice, each ½ lb, cleaned and gutted
4x15ml/4 tbs lemon juice	4 tbs lemon juice
salt, white pepper	salt, white pepper
4x15ml/4 tbs oil	4 tbs oil
1 onion	1 onion
250ml/8 fl oz white wine	1 cup white wine
250ml/8 fl oz hot stock	1 cup hot stock
2½ml/½ tsp sugar	½ tsp sugar
5x15ml/5 tbs cream	5 tbs cream
For the garnish:	
parsley, chopped	parsley, chopped
1 lemon, quartered	1 lemon, quartered
2 tomatoes, sliced	2 tomatoes, sliced

Preheat oven to 220°C/425°F/Gas 7. Rinse the plaice briefly and pat dry. Sprinkle with lemon juice, salt, and pepper. Heat the oil in two frying pans and fry the plaice for 2 mins. each side. Take out and place in an ovenproof dish. Chop the onion, and place in a saucepan with the white wine, stock, and sugar. Stir until the sugar is dissolved. Pour over the fish. Place the dish in a preheated oven on the centre shelf for 10 mins. Then take the plaice out of the oven and carefully stir in the cream. Sprinkle with chopped parsley, and garnish with quarters of lemon and slices of tomato.

In Nice, France's famous seaside resort on the Côte d'Azur, plaice is garnished appetizingly with anchovies and olives.

KETTLE FISH

Preparation time: 50 mins.
About 565 calories/2365 joules
Accompaniments: peas and boiled potatoes, tossed in butter and parsley

If possible, use a fish kettle to poach freshwater fish.
It helps to prevent the fish from breaking.

Metric/Imperial	American
2 plaice, about 500g/1 lb	2 plaice, about 1 lb
500g/1 lb fresh eel	1 lb fresh eel
300g/10 oz haddock	10 oz haddock
(all fish ready cleaned and gutted)	
juice 1 lemon	juice 1 lemon
1 clove garlic	1 clove garlic
1 bay leaf	1 bay leaf
1 sprig each fresh, or 1 tsp each dried, thyme, marjoram, and rosemary	1 sprig each fresh, or 1 tsp each dried, thyme, marjoram, and rosemary
4 sprigs each parsley and dill	4 sprigs each parsley and dill
2 sprigs fresh, or 2 tsp dried chervil	2 sprigs fresh, or 2 tsp dried chervil
125ml/4 fl oz water	½ cup water
250ml/8 fl oz white wine	1 cup white wine
salt, white pepper	salt, white pepper
75g/3 oz butter	6 tbs butter

Wash all the fish and remove bones. Cut in 5½cm/2 in. pieces. Sprinkle with lemon juice. Peel the garlic and cut in half. Rub the inside of a large saucepan with it. Tie the fresh herbs together, or tie the dried herbs in a piece of muslin, and hang into the saucepan with the bay leaf. Add the fish and pour water and wine over. Bring to the boil, then reduce heat and poach gently for 10 mins. Season, add 2 oz/4 tbs butter, and simmer for a further 10 mins. Remove the bay leaf and herbs, and add remaining butter. Pour into a heated serving dish and serve immediately.

TIP
Another way to serve freshwater fish: lard with strips of bacon, sprinkle with lemon juice, and cook in its own juice with some chopped root vegetables, onion, herbs, and a little white wine.

PLAICE NIÇOISE

Preparation time: 35 mins.
About 265 calories/1109 joules
Accompaniments: green salad and garlic bread

Metric/Imperial	American
8 tinned fillets of anchovy	8 canned fillets of anchovy
8 fillets of plaice	8 fillets of plaice
2x15ml/2 tbs lemon juice	2 tbs lemon juice
8 small tomatoes	8 small tomatoes
salt	salt
40g/1½ oz flour	3 tbs flour
6x15ml/6 tbs olive oil	6 tbs olive oil
white pepper, garlic powder	white pepper, garlic powder
8 black olives	8 black olives

Soak the anchovy fillets in water. Sprinkle the fillets of plaice with lemon juice and leave for 10 mins. Skin, quarter, and seed tomatoes.

Season the plaice with salt and roll in flour. Heat the oil in two frying pans and fry the fish for 3 mins. each side. Keep warm on a heated serving plate. Add the tomatoes to the oil and season with salt, pepper, and garlic powder. Cook for 5 mins. Spread over the plaice. Drain the anchovy fillets and slice lengthwise. Halve the olives and remove the stones. Lay 2 strips of anchovy crosswise over each fillet of plaice and arrange slices of olive between each.

BLANKENESE PLAICE

Preparation time: 30 mins.
About 335 calories/1402 joules

Metric/Imperial	American
4 plaice, cleaned and gutted	4 plaice, cleaned and gutted
salt	salt
40g/1½ oz flour	3 tbs flour
40g/1½ oz butter	3 tbs butter
3x15ml/3 tbs oil	3 tbs oil
100g/4 oz button mushrooms	4 oz mushrooms
150g/5 oz prawns	5 oz prawns
2x15ml/2 tbs lemon juice	2 tbs lemon juice
parsley for garnish	parsley for garnish

Rinse the plaice briefly, pat dry, and sprinkle with salt. Roll in flour. Melt a mixture of butter and oil in two frying pans and fry the plaice gently for 6 mins. each side.

In the meantime, prepare the mushrooms and prawns. Slice the mushrooms. Arrange the plaice on a heated serving dish and keep warm.

Add the mushrooms and prawns to the fat in the pans and cook for 5 mins. Spread over the plaice and sprinkle with lemon juice. Garnish with chopped parsley, and serve immediately.

TIP
To make Blankenese plaice even more savoury, fry it in bacon fat with chopped bacon.

Blankenese plaice.

Fried freshwater fish is seasoned with sage and rosemary and cooked in white wine.

FRIED FRESHWATER FISH

Preparation time: 45 mins.
About 270 calories/1130 joules
Accompaniments: green salad and new potatoes

Metric/Imperial	American
750g/1½ lbs freshwater fish (roach, bream, or tench)	1½ lbs freshwater fish (roach, bream, or tench)
juice 1 lemon	juice 1 lemon
salt, white pepper	salt, white pepper
dried sage and rosemary, crumbled	dried sage and rosemary, crumbled
6x15ml/6 tbs oil	6 tbs oil
125ml/4 fl oz white wine	½ cup white wine
juice 1 lemon	juice 1 lemon
For the garnish:	
few sprigs parsley	few sprigs parsley
1 tomato	1 tomato
2 slices lemon	2 slices lemon

Scale the fish and cut open the belly with a sharp knife. Gut, and rinse inside and out. Carefully make three slashes across both sides. Sprinkle with lemon juice. Cover and leave for 10 mins. Then season well inside and out with salt, pepper, crumbled dried sage and rosemary.

Heat the oil in a frying pan and fry the fish for 5 mins. each side. Pour in the white wine and cook gently for a further 5 mins. Arrange on a heated serving plate. Sprinkle with lemon juice. Garnish with parsley sprigs, and tomato and lemon slices.

POACHED FRESHWATER FISH

Preparation time: 50 mins.
About 335 calories/1402 joules
Accompaniments: mixed salad and potatoes tossed in butter and parsley

Metric/Imperial	American
1kg/2¼ lbs freshwater fish (roach, bream, or tench)	2¼ lbs freshwater fish (roach, bream, or tench)
juice 1 lemon	juice 1 lemon
salt	salt
125ml/4 fl oz white wine	½ cup white wine
375ml/12 fl oz water	1½ cups water
1 onion	1 onion
1 bay leaf	1 bay leaf
5 peppercorns	5 peppercorns
2½ml/½ tsp mustard seeds	½ tsp mustard seeds
For the garnish:	
1 lemon	1 lemon
1 tomato	1 tomato
few sprigs dill	few sprigs dill
In addition:	
50g/2 oz butter	4 tbs butter

Freshwater fish belong to the carp family and live, as the name implies, in ponds or small lakes. Bream, roach, and tench are all members of the same family.

Scale the fish, cut open the belly with a sharp knife and gut. Rinse well inside and out. Sprinkle with lemon juice, cover and leave to marinade for 10 mins. Then rub inside and out with salt.

Bring the white wine, water, halved onion, bay leaf, peppercorns, and mustard seeds to the boil in a large saucepan. Add the fish and poach gently for 20 mins. until cooked. Remove with a draining spoon, drain well, and arrange on a heated serving plate. Garnish with lemon and tomato wedges, and sprinkle with chopped dill. Brown the butter in a small pan and serve separately.

ROACH LAUSITZ STYLE

Preparation time without marinading: 1 hr. 20 mins.
About 510 calories/2134 joules

Metric/Imperial

1¼kg/2¾ lbs roach
juice 1 lemon
1 onion
grated rind of 1 lemon
few sprigs parsley
250ml/8 fl oz white wine
  vinegar
flour
2x15ml/2 tbs olive oil
  for frying
For the sauce:
3 onions
6 tomatoes
2x15ml/2 tbs white wine
salt
1 pinch sugar
1 bay leaf
For the garnish:
few sprigs dill, chopped

½ lemon, sliced

American

2¾ lbs roach
juice 1 lemon
1 onion
grated rind of 1 lemon
few sprigs parsley
1 cup white wine
  vinegar
flour
2 tbs olive oil for
  frying

3 onions
6 tomatoes
2 tbs white wine
salt
1 pinch sugar
1 bay leaf

few sprigs dill,
  chopped
½ lemon, sliced

Roach are members of the carp family. They are a vivid orange-red colour. The flesh is full of flavour and tender, but it has a lot of bones.

Preheat oven to 200°C/400°F/Gas 6. Wash the fish. Remove scales with the back of a knife. Make a slit along the belly from head to tail and gut. Rinse inside and out. Drain and sprinkle with lemon juice.

Finely chop the onion. Add the grated lemon rind and chopped parsley. Pour in the vinegar and mix well. Place the fish in the marinade, cover and leave for 2 hrs. Take out, pat dry, and roll in some flour. Heat the oil in a frying pan and fry the roach for 5 mins. on each side. Place the fried fish in a preheated ovenproof dish.

For the sauce, cut the onions into rings. Skin and dice the tomatoes finely. Fry the onion rings in the remaining fat for 3 mins. until transparent. Add the tomatoes. Pour in the white wine, and season with salt, sugar, and bay leaf. Simmer gently for 5 mins. Remove the bay leaf and pour the sauce over the fish. Cover the dish with a lid or foil and place in the preheated oven for 20 mins. Remove the roach from the oven, sprinkle with chopped dill, and garnish with sliced lemon.

Roach Lausitz style is first marinaded, fried, and then baked in a tasty sauce.

RUFF

The ruff is a striking brick-red colour, dotted with dark spots. Once exposed to air, however, even the reddest ruff turns grey. This is caused by the pigments in its skin. It does not mean, however, that its taste deteriorates. A ruff can be recognized by its spiky back fin: this is best removed before scaling.

Ruff can reach a length of 1m/3 ft. Its habitat is in the waters along the Norwegian coasts, in the Barents Sea, and around Iceland. Fillet of ruff is firm, more fatty than cod, for instance, and keeps its shape well in cooking. It is available fresh, frozen or smoked. About ⅔ of the fish is waste, and this is reflected in the price.

RUFF WITH BANANAS

Preparation time: 45 mins.
About 505 calories/2113 joules
Accompaniments: rice and curry sauce

Metric/Imperial	American
4 fillets of ruff, each each 200g/7 oz	4 fillets of ruff, each 7 oz
juice 1 lemon	juice 1 lemon
salt, white pepper	salt, white pepper
50g/2 oz flour	4 tbs flour
oil for deep frying	oil for deep frying
500g/1 lb tomatoes	1 lb tomatoes
4 bananas	4 bananas
juice ½ lemon	juice ½ lemon
4x15ml/4 tbs oil	4 tbs oil
paprika	paprika
1 lemon	1 lemon

Rinse the fillets of ruff and pat dry. Sprinkle with lemon juice, salt, and pepper. Roll in flour.
Heat the oil in a deep fat fryer to 180°C/350°F. Fry the fillets for 8 mins. until golden all over. Take out and drain on kitchen paper. Keep warm.
Skin, seed, and chop the tomatoes. Peel the bananas, cut in half lengthwise, and dice roughly. Sprinkle with lemon juice. Heat the oil in a frying pan and fry the tomato and banana cubes for 5 mins. Season with salt, pepper, and paprika. Arrange on a heated serving plate, place the fish on top, and garnish with lemon wedges.

MAJORCAN RUFF

Preparation time: 1 hr. 10 mins.
About 465 calories/1946 joules
Accompaniment: saffron rice

Metric/Imperial	American
2 aubergines	2 egg plants
1 red and 1 green pepper	1 red and 1 green pepper
250g/8 oz tomatoes	½ lb tomatoes
1 onion	1 onion
5x15ml/5 tbs oil	5 tbs oil
salt, white pepper	salt, white pepper
1 pinch of garlic salt	1 pinch of garlic salt
1 pinch of cayenne pepper	1 pinch of cayenne pepper
4 fillets of ruff, each 200g/7 oz	4 fillets of ruff, each 7 oz
juice 1 lemon	juice 1 lemon
butter for greasing	butter for greasing
125ml/4 fl oz white wine	½ cup white wine
25g/1 oz butter	2 tbs butter
150g/5 oz prawns	5 oz shrimps
few sprigs parsley	few sprigs parsley

Preheat oven to 220°C/425°F/Gas 7. Dice the aubergines/egg plants roughly. Seed and chop the peppers. Skin, seed, and cut the tomatoes in wedges. Chop the onion finely.
Heat the oil in a frying pan, and cook the vegetables for 5 mins. Season with salt, pepper, garlic salt, and cayenne pepper.
Rinse the fillets of ruff and pat dry. Sprinkle with lemon juice, salt, and pepper.'
Grease an ovenproof dish with butter. Insert the fillets and pour over the white wine. Spread the vegetables over the fish and place the dish in the preheated oven for 25 mins.
In the meantime, melt the butter in a frying pan and fry the prawns for 3 mins. Take the ruff out of the oven, and garnish with the prawns and finely chopped parsley.

Filled ruff slices.

FILLED RUFF SLICES

Preparation time: 55 mins.
About 745 calories/3118 joules

Metric/Imperial

4 slices fillets of ruff,
** each 200g/7 oz**
juice 1 lemon
salt, white pepper
4 slices Emmenthal or
** Gouda cheese**
200g/7 oz flour
3 eggs
125ml/4 fl oz light ale
oil for deep frying

American

4 slices fillets of ruff,
** each 7 oz**
juice 1 lemon
salt, white pepper
4 slices Swiss or
** Gouda cheese**
1²/₃ cups flour
3 eggs
½ cup light beer
oil for deep frying

Rinse the fillets of ruff and pat dry. Make a slit sideways into the fish slices to make pockets. Stuff the pockets with lemon juice, salt, pepper, and cheese slices. Fasten with a cocktail stick.

Make a batter with flour, eggs, beer, and salt. Dip the fillets into the batter, making sure they are well coated. Heat the oil in a deep fat fryer to 180°C/350°F. Fry the fish in batter for 8 mins. until golden all over.

SALMON

The salmon lives in all the oceans of the northern hemisphere. Fully grown, it can reach a respectable length of 1.5m/5 ft. The salmon is unusual in that it spawns in fresh water. Embedded in crevices between the pebbles of mountain rivers, the tiny fish hatches and lives in fresh water for two years. Then it leaves its native river and heads for the sea. There, it fattens itself on small herring for three years, while it is also hunted itself by porpoise, shark, and ray.

Towards the end of that time, the salmon begins its long journey back to its native river to spawn. During its strenuous journey across rocks and dams up the river, it does not feed at all, but lives on its fat reserves. At that time it looses its typical silvery colouring: the back becomes a browny blue and the sides turn a pale pink. After spawning the salmon die in large numbers. Most have used up their energy reserves and they die in the river.

At the beginning of spawning time, however, salmon become most interesting for fishing. The tastiest come from the North Sea, but the largest catch areas lie before Alaska and Northwest Canada in the Pacific Ocean.

FRIED SALMON

Preparation time: 30 mins.
About 235 calories/983 joules

Metric/Imperial	American
4 salmon steaks, each 200g/7 oz	4 salmon steaks, each 7 oz
salt	salt
juice 1 lemon	juice 1 lemon
3x15ml/3 tbs flour	3 tbs flour
40g/1½ oz butter	3 tbs butter
125ml/4 fl oz white wine	½ cup white wine
few sprigs parsley, dill	few sprigs parsley, dill
white pepper	white pepper
1 lemon	1 lemon

Rinse the salmon steaks briefly and pat dry. Sprinkle with salt and lemon juice.

Melt the butter in a frying pan, and fry the salmon for 5 mins. each side until brown and crisp. Arrange on a heated serving plate and keep warm.

Stir the flour and white wine into the butter in the frying pan, scraping all the bits at the bottom. Chop parsley and dill finely and add to the sauce. Season with salt and pepper and heat through.

Garnish the fish with the lemon, cut in wedges. Serve the sauce separately.

SALMON DUCHESS ALICE

Preparation time: 1 hr. 30 mins.
About 950 calories/3976 joules

Metric/Imperial	American
1 kg/2¼ lbs salmon in one piece (cut from the middle)	2¼ lbs salmon in one piece (cut from the middle)
500ml/16 fl oz medium white wine	2 cups medium white wine
500ml/16 fl oz water	2 cups water
8 peppercorns	8 peppercorns
1 small bay leaf	1 small bay leaf
salt	salt
1 carrot	1 carrot
few parsley stalks	few parsley stalks
2 sticks celery	2 sticks celery
1 onion	1 onion
For the vol-au-vent filling:	
2 small tomatoes	2 small tomatoes
few sprigs parsley	few sprigs parsley
50g/2 oz butter	4 tbs butter
1x15ml/1 tbs flour	1 tbs flour
125ml/4 fl oz white wine	½ cup white wine
100g/4 oz tinned asparagus tips	4 oz canned asparagus tips
175g/6 oz tinned crabmeat	6 oz canned crabmeat
salt, white pepper	salt, white pepper
In addition:	
4 ready-baked puff pastry cases	4 ready-baked puff pastry cases
100g/4 oz mushrooms	¼ lb mushrooms
25g/1 oz margarine	2 tbs margarine
6x15ml/6 tbs cream	6 tbs cream
2 egg yolks	2 egg yolks
oil for deep frying	oil for deep frying
For the batter:	
75g/3 oz flour	⅔ cup flour
6x15ml/6 tbs milk	6 tbs milk
1 egg	1 egg
12 fresh or smoked oysters	12 fresh or smoked oysters
½ punnet mustard and cress	½ punnet cress

Preheat oven to 220°C/425°F/Gas 7. Rinse the salmon briefly, and pat dry. Bring the wine and water to the boil with the peppercorns, bay leaf, and a good pinch of salt. Roughly chop the carrot, parsley, and celery. Slice the onion. Spread over the bottom of a wide casserole and lay the fish on top. Pour the liquor over, cover, and place in the preheated oven on the centre shelf for 30 mins.

The puff pastry cases served with Salmon Duchess Alice are filled with crabmeat and asparagus tips.

In the meantime, skin, seed, and roughly chop the tomatoes. Chop the parsley. Melt the butter in a saucepan and stir in the flour. Pour in the white wine and cook for 5 mins. Then add the tomatoes, parsley, drained asparagus tips, and flaked crabmeat. Season with salt and pepper. Keep warm but do not boil. Remove the salmon from the oven, and drain. Arrange on a heated serving dish and keep warm. Reserve the liquor.

Reduce the oven heat to 180°C/350°F/Gas 4.

Put the puff pastry cases on a baking tray, and place in the oven on the centre shelf for 12 mins.

Pour the fish liquor through a strainer and reduce to a third by boiling hard. Slice the mushrooms thinly. Melt the margarine in a small saucepan and cook them for 5 mins. Add to the fish liquor, and simmer for a further 5 mins. Mix the cream with the egg yolks, and stir into the sauce. Heat through but do not boil. Keep warm.

Heat the oil in a deep fat fryer to 180°C/350°F.

Make a batter with the flour, milk, and egg. Season with salt. Leave to rest for 5 mins. Dip the shelled oysters (or drained smoked) oysters in the batter, and fry in the hot oil for about 5 mins. Drain on kitchen paper. Remove the pastry cases from the oven and fill with the crabmeat mixture. Garnish with mustard and cress. Arrange on the serving dish, and place the oysters in between. Pour a little mushroom sauce over the salmon, and serve the rest separately.

BARBECUED SALMON WITH ANCHOVY BUTTER

Preparation time: 45 mins.
About 530 calories/2218 joules

Metric/Imperial	American
4 salmon steaks, each 200g/8 oz	4 salmon steaks, each ½ lb
salt, white pepper	salt, white pepper
1 onion	1 onion
few sprigs parsley	few sprigs parsley
5x15ml/5 tbs oil	5 tbs oil
2x15ml/2 tbs lemon juice	2 tbs lemon juice
100g/4 oz anchovy butter, chilled	¼ cup anchovy butter, chilled
2 lemons	2 lemons

Rinse the salmon steaks and pat dry. Season with salt and pepper and place in a dish. Slice the onion thinly and put on top of the fish. Chop the parsley, reserving 4 sprigs for garnish, and sprinkle over the fish. Mix the oil with the lemon juice and pour over the fish. Leave to marinade for 15 mins., turning occasionally. Remove the onion and parsley and discard. Take the salmon steaks out of the marinade and place on the grid of a hot barbecue or under a preheated grill. Grill for 6 mins. each side, basting occasionally with the marinade.

Slice the anchovy butter thinly and place ⅔ of it on a serving plate. Arrange the salmon steaks on top and cover with the remaining anchovy butter. Garnish the salmon with the reserved sprigs of parsley and wedges of lemon.

Salmon with almond sauce.

SALMON WITH ALMOND SAUCE

Preparation time: 60 mins.
About 500 calories/2093 joules

Metric/Imperial	American
For the fish:	
4 salmon steaks, each 200g/7 oz	4 salmon steaks, each 7 oz
juice ½ lemon	juice ½ lemon
salt, white pepper	salt, white pepper
2 onions	2 onions
50g/2 oz butter or margarine	4 tbs butter or margarine
6x15ml/6 tbs hot stock made from cubes	½ cup hot stock made from cubes
1 bay leaf	1 bay leaf
For the sauce:	
1 stale bread roll, without the crust	1 stale bread roll, without the crust
3x15ml/3 tbs milk	3 tbs milk
125g/4 oz ground almonds	1 cup ground almonds
1 clove garlic	1 clove garlic
salt	salt
2x15ml/2 tbs water	2 tbs water
grated nutmeg	grated nutmeg
2x15ml/2 tbs vinegar	2 tbs vinegar
2x15ml/2 tbs oil	2 tbs oil
1 pinch of sugar	1 pinch of sugar
1 egg yolk	1 egg yolk
2x15ml/2 tbs cream	2 tbs cream
parsley for garnish	parsley for garnish

Preheat oven to 220°C/425°F/Gas 7. Rinse the salmon steaks and pat dry. Sprinkle with lemon juice, salt, and pepper. Slice the onions thinly. Melt the butter or margarine in a shallow, ovenproof pan and fry the onions for 5 mins. until golden. Place the fish on top of the onions and pour over the hot stock. Add the bay leaf, cover, and poach gently for 15 mins.

For the sauce, soak the bread roll in milk. Crush the garlic with salt and mix with the ground almonds and water. Squeeze dry the bread roll and stir into the almond mixture. Season with nutmeg and salt and mix in the vinegar and oil. Beat the egg yolk with the cream and sugar and add to the mixture.

Remove the bay leaf from the fish pan and pour the sauce over the fish. Place in the preheated oven on the centre shelf for 10 mins.

When a brown crust is formed on the fish, garnish the dish with chopped parsley and serve immediately.

SALMON ST. GERMAIN

Preparation time: 55 mins.
About 1015 calories/4249 joules

Metric/Imperial

For the noisette potatoes:
1½kg/3½ lbs potatoes
100g/4 oz butter
For the salmon:
40g/1½ oz stale white
   bread, without the
   crusts
75g/3 oz butter
4 fillets of salmon, each
   200g/7 oz
juice 1 lemon
salt, white pepper
few sprigs parsley
1 lemon
1 jar of Béarnaise sauce

American

3½ lbs potatoes
½ cup butter

2 slices stale white
   bread, without the
   crusts
⅓ cup butter
4 fillets of salmon, each
   7 oz
juice 1 lemon
salt, white pepper
few sprigs parsley
1 lemon
1 jar of Béarnaise sauce

Peel potatoes, wash, and drain. With a melon baller, scoop out nut-size balls. Boil in salted water for 5 mins. Drain. Melt the butter in a frying pan. Fry the potato balls for 20 mins. until golden.

In the meantime, prepare the salmon. Crumb the white bread finely. Melt the butter until liquid but not hot. Rinse the fillets of salmon and pat dry. Sprinkle on both sides with lemon juice, salt, and pepper. First dip in the melted butter and then roll in the breadcrumbs. Heat remaining butter in a frying pan and fry the fillets for 5 mins. each side. Arrange on a heated serving plate. Surround with the browned potato balls, and garnish with sprigs of parsley and wedges of lemon. Carefully heat the Béarnaise sauce over a pan of hot water. Serve immediately with the salmon.

Salmon St. Germain.

Salmon Lafayette is garnished with prawns and truffles.

SALMON LAFAYETTE

Preparation time: 40 mins.
About 290 calories/1214 joules

Metric/Imperial	American
125g/4 oz prawns	¼ lb shrimps
500ml/16 fl oz water	2 cups water
6x15ml/6 tbs white wine	½ cup white wine
salt, white pepper	salt, white pepper
1 carrot, 1 onion,	1 carrot, 1 onion,
1 celery stalk, 1 leek	1 celery stalk, 1 leek
4 salmon steaks,	4 salmon steaks,
each 200g/7 oz	each 7 oz
For the sauce:	
250ml/8 fl oz fish liquor	1 cup fish liquor
125ml/4 fl oz white wine	½ cup white wine
salt, white pepper	salt, white pepper
1 egg yolk	1 egg yolk
1x15ml/1 tbs tomato purée	1 tbs tomato paste
40g/1½ oz butter	3 tbs butter
1x5ml/1 tsp cornflour	1 tsp cornstarch
½ tin truffles (25g/1 oz)	½ can truffles (1 oz)

Prepare the prawns. Chop the vegetables and bring to the boil with the water, white wine, salt, and pepper. Wash the salmon steaks and add to the liquor. Poach gently for 15 mins. until cooked. Take out of the liquor with a draining spoon and keep warm on a heated serving plate.

Strain the fish liquor, measure out about 250ml/8 fl oz/1 cup and reduce to half by boiling steadily.

Add the white wine and season with salt and pepper. Mix the egg yolk with the tomato purée and stir into the sauce. Keep hot, but do not allow to boil. Whisk in the butter in small flakes until the sauce become slightly frothy. Mix the cornflour with a little water and stir into the sauce. Heat remaining fish liquor, add the prawns, and gently warm in the liquor. Drain the truffles and chop roughly.

Surround the salmon steaks with the prawns. Pour the sauce over the fish, garnish with chopped truffles, and serve immediately.

LEMON SALMON

Preparation time: 50 mins.
About 290 calories/1214 joules
Accompaniments: cauliflower and sautéed potatoes

Metric/Imperial	American
250ml/8 fl oz white wine	1 cup white wine
125ml/4 fl oz hot stock	½ cup hot stock
1 onion	1 onion
1 bay leaf	1 bay leaf
3 cloves	3 cloves
few sprigs parsley	few sprigs parsley
1 sprig fresh or ½ tsp	1 sprig fresh or ½ tsp
dried tarragon	dried tarragon
peel of ¼ lemon	peel of ¼ lemon
1 pinch of sugar	1 pinch of sugar
salt	salt
4 salmon steaks,	4 salmon steaks,
each 200g/7 oz	each 7 oz
For the sauce:	
75g/3 oz butter	⅓ cup butter
2 egg yolks	2 egg yolks
3x15ml/3 tbs lemon juice	3 tbs lemon juice
salt	salt
1x5ml/1 tsp cornflour	1 tsp cornstarch
For the garnish:	
few sprigs parsley	few sprigs parsley
4 lemon slices	4 lemon slices

Boil the white wine and hot stock together in a saucepan. Spike the onion with cloves and pieces of bay leaf. Add to the liquor with the parsley, tarragon, lemon peel, sugar, and salt. Cover and simmer for 10 mins. Rinse the salmon steaks, place in the liquor, and poach gently for 15 mins. Take out, drain, and arrange on a preheated serving plate. Cover and keep warm.

Strain the fish liquor. Stir in the butter teaspoon by teaspoon. Mix the egg yolks with the lemon juice, salt, and cornflour and gradually add to the sauce. Pour over the salmon and place under a preheated grill to brown for 3 mins. Garnish with parsley sprigs and lemon slices. For a cheaper version of this dish, substitute cod steaks and prepare in the same way.

GRAVLAX

Pickled salmon

Preparation time without marinading: 45 mins.
About 645 calories/2699 joules

Metric/Imperial	American
1 piece of salmon (centre cut), about 1kg/2¼ lbs	1 piece of salmon (centre cut), about 2¼ lbs
100g/4 oz fresh or 5 tbs dried dill	4 oz fresh or 5 tbs dried dill
1x15ml/1 tbs white peppercorns	1 tbs white peppercorns
3x15ml/3 tbs sugar	3 tbs sugar
4x15ml/4 tbs salt	4 tbs salt
For the sauce:	
3x15ml/3 tbs prepared mustard	3 tbs hot mustard
1x15ml/1 tsp mustard powder	1 tsp mustard powder
3x15ml/3 tbs sugar	3 tbs sugar
1x15ml/1 tbs white wine vinegar	1 tbs white wine vinegar
3x15ml/3 tbs pickling liquor	3 tbs pickling liquor

Scale the fish, if necessary, under cold water, and pat dry. Cut in half and carefully remove all bones. Lay one half, skin-side down, in a shallow dish. Cover with dill, and sprinkle with coarsley ground white peppercorns, sugar, and salt. Lay the other half of fish on top, skin-side up. Cover with aluminium foil. Place and plate or lid on top and weigh down with some tins or similar. Pour over the pickling liquor and turn occasionally. Keep in a cool place (not the refrigerator) for at least 48 hrs. Remove the salmon from the pickling liquor, wipe, and arrange on a wooden board.

For the sauce, mix the mustard with the mustard powder, sugar, and vinegar. Slowly pour in the pickling liquor and whisk to a creamy sauce. Serve this sauce separately.

When it is pickled in a spicy marinade, the Swedes and Danes call their salmon Gravlax. This dish is absolutely delicious.

SARDINES

What we call sardines are really pilchards, as sardines are the young fish. Fully grown, they can reach a length of 25cm/10 ins., and then they are hardly discernible from herring. Sardines are caught near the coasts of Italy, Spain, Portugal, France, and America.

Sardines are most familiar to us when they are gutted and beheaded and packed tightly in oval shaped tins, either in oil or in brine. Fresh sardines, however, have an excellent, quite different, flavour. They are the larger pilchards, and are popular in Portuguese, Spanish, and Italian cuisine. The Spanish and Portuguese often fry them over charcoal on folk festivals.

Sometimes fresh sardines are available at fishmongers, and frozen fish can usually be obtained easily.

ARLES SARDINES

Preparation time: 45 mins.
About 195 calories/816 joules

Metric/Imperial	American
1 cucumber	1 cucumber
250ml/8 fl oz water	1 cup water
3 white peppercorns	3 white peppercorns
1 bay leaf	1 bay leaf
salt, pinch of sugar	salt, pinch of sugar
juice ½ lemon	juice ½ lemon
4x15ml/4 tbs olive oil	4 tbs olive oil
375g/12 oz fresh sardines if available or tinned sardines in oil	12 oz fresh sardines if available or canned sardines in oil
125g/4 oz tomatoes	¼ lb tomatoes
1 large onion	1 large onion
garlic powder	garlic powder
1x15ml/1 tbs lemon juice	1 tbs lemon juice
parsley for garnish	parsley for garnish

Peel the cucumber and cut in half lengthwise. Remove the seeds with a spoon and cut cucumber in 2½cm/1 in. cubes.

Add the peppercorns, bay leaf, salt, and sugar to the water, bring to the boil, and simmer for 5 mins. Remove the peppercorns and bay leaf, and add the lemon juice and oil. Insert the cucumber cubes, marinade for 20 mins., drain, and cool. Drain the oil off the sardines if using tinned ones, and arrange the fish on a serving plate. Surround with the cucumber.

Skin, seed, and finely dice the tomatoes. Dice the onion. Place both over the sardines. Season with garlic powder, and sprinkle with lemon juice and chopped parsley.

In Arles in France, sardines are served with cooked cucumber, tomatoes and onions.

SHARK STEAK GRENOBLE STYLE

Preparation time: 30 mins.
About 495 calories/2072 joules

Metric/Imperial	American
4 shark steaks, each 250g/8 oz	4 shark steaks, each ½ lb
juice 1 lemon	juice 1 lemon
salt, garlic salt	salt, garlic salt
40g/1½ oz flour	3 tbs flour
oil for frying	oil for frying
40g/1½ oz butter	3 tbs butter
1x15ml/1 tbs capers	1 tbs capers
juice ½ lemon	juice ½ lemon
few sprigs parsley	few sprigs parsley
125ml/4 fl oz dry white wine	½ cup dry white wine
1x15ml/1 tbs sugar	1 tbs sugar
For the garnish:	
1 lemon, quartered	1 lemon, quartered
2 sprigs fresh dill	2 sprigs fresh dill

Very occasionally, one can find shark at the fishmonger. It has usually been caught in the nets by accident when fishing for other fish. Sharks attain a length of up to 1m/3 ft, and are available as steaks or cutlets. The flesh has a mild and delicate taste and is well worth trying.

Rinse the shark steaks and pat dry. Sprinkle with lemon juice, cover, and leave for 15 mins. Season with salt and garlic salt. Roll in flour. Heat the oil in a large frying pan and fry the steaks for 3 mins. on each side. Place on a serving dish and keep warm. Melt the butter in the frying pan. Chop the capers, add to the butter with the lemon juice, and cook for 2 mins. Chop the parsley finely, and add to the sauce. Pour in the wine and stir in the sugar. Reduce the sauce a little by boiling and pour over the shark steaks. Garnish with a slice of lemon on top of each steak and chopped dill.

FRICASSÉE OF PRAWNS AU GRATIN

Preparation time: 25 mins.
About 265 calories/1109 joules

Metric/Imperial	American
200g/7 oz prawns	7 oz shrimps
100g/4 oz tinned asparagus tips	4 oz canned asparagus tips
25g/1 oz butter	2 tbs butter
1x15ml/1 tsp flour	1 tsp flour
salt, white pepper	salt, white pepper
grated nutmeg	grated nutmeg
2 egg yolks	2 egg yolks
125ml/ 4 fl oz cream	½ cup cream
40g/1½ oz Emmenthal cheese, grated	3 tbs Swiss cheese, grated
butter for greasing	butter for greasing
3x15ml/3 tbs dried breadcrumbs	3 tbs dried breadcrumbs
1x15ml/1 tbs butter	1 tbs butter

Preheat oven to 220°C/425°F/Gas 7. Prepare the prawns. Drain the asparagus tips, reserving the liquid. Melt the butter in a saucepan and stir in the flour. Cook for 5 mins., stirring constantly. Make up the asparagus liquid to 250ml/8 fl oz/1 cup with water and stir into the roux. Season with salt, pepper, and nutmeg and cook for 5 mins. Mix the egg yolks with a little of the sauce and add to the saucepan. Stir in the cream and cheese, and heat, but do not boil. Fold in the prawns and drained asparagus tips.

Grease an ovenproof dish with butter. Pour in the fricassée. Sprinkle with dried breadcrumbs and dot with butter. Place in the preheated oven on the upper shelf for 3 mins.

Fricassée of prawns au gratin.

CHILLI SHRIMPS

Preparation time: 30 mins.
About 380 calories/1590 joules
Accompaniments: boiled rice and white wine

Metric/Imperial	American
300g/10 oz frozen shrimps	10 oz frozen shrimps
1 large onion	1 large onion
1x15ml/1 tbs oil	1 tbs oil
4 tomatoes	4 tomatoes
300g/10 oz tinned haricot beans	10 oz canned white navy beans
2½ml/½ tsp garlic salt	½ tsp garlic salt
2½ml/½ tsp chilli powder	½ tsp chilli powder
1x5ml/1 tsp oregano	1 tsp oregano
1¼ml/¼ tsp ground caraway seeds	¼ tsp ground caraway seeds
dill for garnish	dill for garnish

Defrost the shrimps. Chop the onion finely, and fry in hot oil until golden. Skin and chop the tomatoes roughly. Add to the onion, together with the shrimps, drained beans, and the herbs and spices. Mix well. Cook gently for 15 mins. until the shrimps are cooked. Do not boil as this might make the shrimps tough. Serve garnished with dill.

CRAYFISH TAILS WITH ASPARAGUS

Queues d'écrevisse aux asperges

Preparation time: 1 hr 25 mins.
About 450 calories/1883 joules

Metric/Imperial	American
2 litres/3½ pints water	9 cup water
salt	salt
3 peppercorns	3 peppercorns
juice ½ lemon	juice ½ lemon
20 live crayfish, each 100g/4 oz	20 live crayfish, each 4 oz

For the Hollandaise sauce:	
250g/8 oz tinned asparagus tips	8 oz canned asparagus tips
150g/5 oz butter	⅔ cup butter
3 egg yolks	3 egg yolks
3x15ml/3 tbs water	3 tbs water
salt, white pepper	salt, white pepper
1 pinch of cayenne pepper	1 pinch of cayenne pepper
1x15ml/1 tbs lemon juice	1 tbs lemon juice
In addition:	
25g/1 oz crayfish or prawn butter, if available	2 tbs crayfish or prawn butter, if available

Chilli shrimps.

Drain the asparagus tips. Melt the butter until liquid but not hot. Whisk the egg yolks with the water in a bowl over a pan of hot water until thick and frothy. Remove from the heat and stir in the melted butter spoon by spoon. Season with salt, pepper, cayenne pepper, and lemon juice. Add the drained asparagus tips. Pour into a heated serving dish. Place the crayfish tails on top. Melt the crayfish or prawn butter and sprinkle over the fish.

NOTE:
The meat from the pincers could be frozen and used later in a salad. Or it could be used with the remaining crayfish meat in the sauce. In that case, only 10 whole crayfish would be needed.

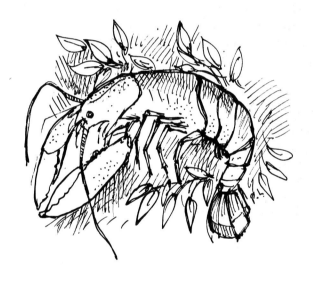

From the classic French cuisine: crayfish tails with asparagus.

Bring the water with salt, peppercorns, and lemon juice to the boil in a large saucepan. Thoroughly wash the crayfish and plunge them head first into the boiling water. Boil for 5 mins., then reduce the heat and poach for a further 15 mins. Drain the crayfish, break off the pincers, and crack open. Remove the flesh. Break off the tails from the body and split sideways. Take off the lid covering the tail and remove the threadlike intestine. Lift out the meat and carefully remove the strip of chitin. Keep the crayfish flesh warm.

Lobster Américaine.

LOBSTER AMÉRICAINE

Preparation time: 50 mins.
About 530 calories/2218 joules
Accompaniments: buttered toast or boiled rice

Metric/Imperial	American
For 6 persons	
3 litres/5 pints salted water	6 pints salted water
2 lobsters, about 1kg/2¼ lbs	2 lobsters, about 2¼ lbs
60g/2½ oz butter	5 tbs butter
6x15ml/6 tbs olive oil	6 tbs olive oil
2 shallots	2 shallots
1 clove garlic	1 clove garlic
4x15ml/4 tbs warmed cognac	4 tbs warmed brandy
500ml/16 fl oz white wine	2 cups white wine
500g/1 lb tomatoes	1 lb tomatoes
salt, white pepper	salt, white pepper
pinch of sugar	pinch of sugar
pinch of cayenne pepper	pinch of cayenne pepper
2x5ml/2 tsp meat extract	2 tsp meat extract
few sprigs parsley	few sprigs parsley
3 sprigs tarragon	3 sprigs tarragon

Bring the salted water to the boil in a large saucepan. Plunge the lobsters head first into the bubbling hot water, and boil for 10 mins. Remove from the water and twist off the tails. Cut in diagonal slices. Crack the claws. Lay the lobster on its back and split it lengthwise down the middle. Remove the stomach and discard. Take out the meat and the green lobster liver. Mix the liver with 25g/1 oz butter in a bowl.

Melt the remaining butter in the oil in a saucepan. Sauté the lobster meat for 5 mins. Chop the shallots finely, and crush the garlic with a little salt. Add to the lobster meat. Pour in the warmed cognac and ignite it. When the flames die down, pour in the white wine. Add the skinned, seeded, and chopped tomatoes. Season was salt, pepper, sugar, and cayenne pepper. Cover, and simmer for 20 mins. Remove the lobster meat and keep warm on a heated serving dish. Stir the meat extract into the sauce. Chop the parsley and tarragon, and add to the sauce with the lobster liver. Correct the seasoning, and pour the sauce over the lobster meat.

LOBSTER THERMIDOR

Preparation time: 1 hr. 10 mins.
About 550 calories/2302 joules
Accompaniments: boiled rice and buttered peas

Metric/Imperial	American
3 litres/5 pints salted water	6 pints salted water
3 lobsters, each 600g/1¼ lbs	3 lobsters, each 1¼ lbs
2 shallots	2 shallots
25g/1 oz butter	2 tbs butter
250ml/8 fl oz white wine	1 cup white wine
2x15ml/2 tbs flour	2 tbs flour
3x15ml/3 tbs lobster water	3 tbs lobster water
salt, white pepper	salt, white pepper
1x5ml/1 tsp prepared mustard	1 tsp hot mustard
250ml/8 fl oz cream	1 cup cream
50g/2 oz Emmenthal cheese, grated	4 tbs Swiss cheese, grated
25g/1 oz butter	2 tbs butter
For the garnish:	
1 round lettuce	1 round lettuce
few sprigs dill	few sprigs dill

Preheat oven to 250°C/475°F/Gas 9. Bring the salted water to the boil. Plunge the lobsters in head first. Boil for 30 mins., drain, and cool. Reserve the liquor.

Split the lobsters lengthwise down the middle. Remove the meat from the body and slice diagonally (reserve the shells). Remove the claw meat, too. Dice roughly.

Chop the shallots finely. Melt the butter in a saucepan and fry the shallots until golden. Pour in the white wine and boil rapidly to reduce to almost nothing. Mix the flour with 3x15ml/3 tbs lobster water, and stir into the sauce. Cook for 3 mins. Season with salt, pepper, and mustard. Stir in the cream. Remove from the heat and add the claw meat. Fill the empty lobster shells with the sauce and cover with the lobster meat slices. Sprinkle with cheese and dot with butter.

Place in the preheated oven on the centre shelf for 15 mins., or place under a preheated grill.

Arrange a bed of lettuce leaves on a serving plate, place the lobster shells on top, and garnish with dill.

Lobster thermidor.

SCAMPI

Scampi are small, deep-sea crayfish, and are related to the lobster. They live in depths of up to 400m/1312 ft in the Mediterranean, mainly near the coasts of Spain and Italy. There, they are usually available fresh, in which case they are prepared like lobster. The claw meat of scampi, however, is so dry that only the tail meat is really enjoyable. We can usually obtain scampi frozen, either whole or shelled. They are also available preserved in tins.

TIP

Scampi tails are sometimes available fresh or cooked at the fishmonger. Important: fresh scampi tails must have light, almost transparent flesh, while cooked ones should be whitish-pink and must not show any dark patches.

Scampi Lacroix.

SCAMPI COSTA BRAVA

Preparation time: 1 hr. 35 mins.
About 335 calories/1402 joules

Metric/Imperial	American
500g/1 lb whole fresh or frozen scampi	1 lb whole fresh or frozen scampi
1 litre/1¾ pts salted water	4½ cups salted water
few sprigs parsley	few sprigs parsley
150g/5 oz mushrooms	2½ cups mushrooms
40g/1½ oz butter	3 tbs butter
salt, white pepper	salt, white pepper
margarine for greasing	margarine for greasing
2 small onions	2 small onions
1 clove garlic	1 clove garlic
250g/8 oz tomatoes	½ lb tomatoes
4x15ml/4 tbs oil	4 tbs oil
2½ml/½ tsp dried basil	½ tsp dried basil
2x15ml/2 tbs tomato ketchup	2 tbs tomato ketchup
25g/1 oz Parmesan cheese, grated	2 tbs Parmesan cheese, grated
1x15ml/1 tbs dried breadcrumbs	1 tbs dried breadcrumbs

Preheat oven to 220°C/425°F/Gas 7. If using frozen scampi defrost according to instructions on the packet. Bring the salted water to the boil, and add the scampi and half of the parsley (reserve the other half). Boil for 5 mins. Remove the scampi with a draining spoon, drain, and cool. Shell the scampi and remove the black thread of intestine. Slice the mushrooms thinly, and fry in butter for 5 mins. Season.

Grease an ovenproof dish and layer the scampi and mushrooms inside. Chop the onions and garlic finely. Skin, seed, and dice the tomatoes. Heat half the oil in the frying pan and fry the onions and garlic for 3 mins. until transparent. Add the tomatoes and season with salt, pepper, and basil. Cover, and cook gently for 5 mins. Stir in the tomato ketchup and pour the sauce over the scampi. Chop the remaining parsley finely, mix with Parmesan cheese and breadcrumbs, and sprinkle evenly over the scampi. Spoon the remaining oil over, and place the dish in the preheated oven on the centre shelf for 10 mins.

SCAMPI LACROIX

Preparation time: 55 mins.
About 350 calories/1465 joules

Metric/Imperial

500g/1 lb fresh or frozen
    scampi
1½ litres/2½ pints salted
    water
3 sprigs dill
2 small onions
100g/4 oz mushrooms
1 small red pepper
60g/2½ oz butter
salt
freshly ground white
    pepper
2x5ml/3 tsp dried mixed
    herbs
4x15ml/4 tbs brandy
1x5ml/1 tsp curry powder
125ml/4 fl oz cream
1 egg yolk

American

1 lb fresh or frozen
    scampi
6¼ cups salted water
3 sprigs dill
2 small onions
¼ lb mushrooms
1 small red pepper
5 tbs butter
salt
freshly ground white
    pepper
2 tsp dried mixed
    herbs
4 tbs brandy
1 tsp curry powder
½ cup cream
1 egg yolk

If necessary defrost scampi according to instructions on the packet. Bring the salted water with the dill to the boil and add the scampi. Poach for 1 min. Remove scampi and drain.

Chop the onions finely, and slice the mushrooms thinly. Seed the red pepper, and cut in small cubes. Melt the butter in a frying pan and fry the scampi for 3 mins. on all sides. Remove and keep warm.

Fry the onions until transparent, add the mushrooms and pepper and fry for 5 mins., stirring occasionally. Season well with salt, pepper, and mixed herbs. Put the scampi back in the pan, warm the brandy, and pour over the scampi. Ignite immediately. When the flames have died down, sprinkle with curry powder and stir in the cream. Simmer for 2 mins. Mix the egg yolk with a little water. Take the pan off the heat. Push the scampi and mushrooms to one side, and pour the egg yolk in the middle. Stir well. Reheat gently, but do not boil. Place on a heated serving dish and serve immediately.

Scampi Costa Brava.

SOLE

Soles are considered to be the best of the flat fish. Sadly, however, they are also the most expensive. Soles take their name from their shoe-like shape. They are mainly caught in the North Sea, but they can also be found along the coasts of the western countries of the Mediterranean and North-West Africa.

The ideal weight of soles is about 300g/10 oz, and they should be treated delicately in the kitchen. Only then do they develop their incomparable flavour. Soles are rarely fried but are usually poached. Cold fillets of sole are an attraction on a cold buffet table.

Sole is usually available ready cleaned and gutted. However, you could gut it quite easily yourself if necessary: make a small cross cut behind the head on the dark side of the fish. Pull out the inside through the resulting opening. Cut off the head, and make an incision at the base of the tail. Take a firm grip on the loosened skin with a piece of kitchen paper, and pull off the skin in the direction of the head. Trim the fins with scissors and rinse the fish briefly.

To fillet the fish, cut along the backbone down the entire length of the fish. Use the natural markings as a guide. Slide a knife under the flesh and remove the fillets with long sweeping strokes. You will now have two fillets. Turn the fish over and repeat the process. Pat dry with kitchen paper and use according to our recipes.

DUTCH SOLE

Preparation time: 30 mins.
About 370 calories/1548 joules

Metric/Imperial	American
8 fillets of sole, each 50g/2 oz	8 fillets of sole, each 2 oz
juice 1 lemon	juice 1 lemon
500ml/16 fl oz water	2 cups water
salt, white pepper	salt. white pepper
For the sauce:	
2 egg yolks	2 egg yolks
1x15ml/1 tbs lemon juice	1 tbs lemon juice
2x15ml/2 tbs water	2 tbs water
salt, white pepper	salt, white pepper
150g/5 oz butter	⅔ cup butter
For the garnish:	
few sprigs parsley	few sprigs parsley
1 lemon	1 lemon

Dry the fillets of sole and sprinkle with some lemon juice. Cover, and leave for 10 mins. Bring the water and the remaining lemon juice to the boil, add salt, and poach the fillets gently for 5 mins. Drain, and sprinkle with pepper. Keep warm.

For the sauce, beat the egg yolks with lemon juice and water. Season with salt and pepper. Place over a saucepan of simmering water and whisk until light and frothy. Gradually add the butter spoon by spoon. Check the seasoning. Arrange the fillets of sole on a heated serving plate, and garnish with sprigs of parsley and lemon wedges. Serve the sauce separately.

NOTE:
Instead of the sauce, you could just serve melted butter.

Dutch sole is served with a classic Hollandaise sauce.

SOLE JAVANESE STYLE

Preparation time: 45 mins.
About 525 calories/2197 joules
Accompaniments: green salad and buttered rice

Metric/Imperial

4 soles, each 250g/8 oz,
 ready cleaned and
 gutted
250ml/8 fl oz water
250ml/8 fl oz white wine
½ bay leaf
2 cloves
salt, white pepper

For the sauce:
25g/1 oz butter
25g/1 oz flour
375ml/12 fl oz hot stock
125ml/4 fl oz cream
salt, pinch of sugar
1x15ml/1 tbs curry
 powder
1x15ml/1 tbs lemon juice

In addition:
2 bananas
25g/1 oz butter
curry powder to taste
2x15ml/2 tbs mango
 chutney
4 puff pastry fleurons

American

4 soles, each ½ lb,
 ready cleaned and
 gutted
1 cup water
1 cup white wine
½ bay leaf
2 cloves
salt, white pepper

2 tbs butter
2 tbs flour
1½ cups hot stock
½ cup cream
salt, pinch of sugar
1 tbs curry powder

1 tbs lemon juice

2 bananas
2 tbs butter
curry powder to taste
2 tbs mango chutney

4 puff pastry fleurons

Rinse the soles and pat dry. Bring the water, wine, bay leaf, and cloves to the boil in a saucepan. Season, add the soles, and poach gently for 10 mins.

In the meantime, for the sauce, melt the butter in a saucepan. Stir in the flour and cook for 3 mins. Gradually add the stock and simmer gently for 5 mins. Remove the pan from the heat and stir in the cream. Season with salt, sugar, curry powder, and lemon juice. Cover and keep warm.

Peel the bananas and halve lengthwise. Melt the butter in a frying pan and fry the bananas for 3 mins. on each side. Sprinkle with curry powder. Add the mango chutney and heat gently.

Remove the soles from the liquor and drain well. Arrange on a heated serving plate. Pour over the curry sauce and lay the bananas on top. Heat the fleurons in a hot oven and use for garnish.

In Java, sole is served with fried
bananas and mango chutney.
It is accompanied with a savoury curry sauce.

Sole Altona.

SOLE ALTONA

Preparation time: 40 mins.
About 535 calories/2239 joules
Accompaniments: green salad and potatoes tossed in
butter and parsley

Metric/Imperial	American
150g/5 oz shelled frozen scampi	5 oz shelled frozen scampi
12 fillets of sole, each 50g/2 oz	12 fillets of sole, each 2 oz
juice 1½ lemons	juice 1½ lemons
250g/8 oz mushrooms	½ lb mushrooms
75g/3 oz butter	⅓ cup butter
150g/5 oz mussels in brine (jar)	5 oz mussels in brine (jar)
salt, cayenne pepper	salt, cayenne pepper
4x15ml/4 tbs flour	4 tbs flour
few sprigs parsley	few sprigs parsley
40g/1½ oz butter	3 tbs butter

If necessary defrost the scampi according to the instructions on the packet. Pat the soles dry, sprinkle with most of the lemon juice, and leave for 10 mins.

In the meantime, quarter the large mushrooms, halve the small ones. Melt 25g/1 oz of butter in a saucepan, and fry the mushrooms for 8 mins. Add the drained mussels and scampi and cook gently for 5 mins. Season with the remaining lemon juice, salt, and cayenne pepper. Keep warm. Sprinkle the fillets of sole with salt and roll in flour. Melt the remaining butter in a frying pan and fry the fillets for 3 mins. each side until golden. Arrange on a heated serving plate. Cover with the mushroom mixture, and sprinkle with finely chopped parsley. Brown the butter and pour over the fish.

SOLE FILLETS IN PRAWN SAUCE

Preparation time: 45 mins.
About 355 calories/1486 joules

Metric/Imperial	American
8 fillets of sole, each 50g/2 oz	8 fillets of sole, each 2 oz
juice ½ lemon	juice ½ lemon
salt, white pepper	salt, white pepper
1x15ml/1 tbs butter for greasing	1 tbs butter for greasing
125ml/4 fl oz white wine	½ cup white wine
For the sauce:	
2x15ml/2 tbs flour	2 tbs flour
250ml/8 fl oz cream	1 cup cream
150g/5 oz prawns	5 oz shrimps
150g/5 oz mushrooms	2½ cups mushrooms
Worcester sauce	Worcester sauce

Preheat oven to 200°C/400°F/Gas 6. Dry the fillets of sole and sprinkle with lemon juice. Cover and leave for 10 mins. Season, then roll up and fasten with wooden cocktail sticks.

Grease an ovenproof dish with butter. Place the fish rolls inside and pour over the white wine. Cover with a lid or foil and place in the preheated oven on the centre shelf for 10 mins.

For the sauce, mix the flour with the cream in a saucepan, and gently warm, stirring continuously. Slice the mushrooms, and add with the prepared prawns to the sauce. Cook gently for 5 mins. Season with Worcester sauce.

Remove the fish rolls from the oven. Carefully pour off the fish liquor, and stir it into the prawn sauce. Pour the sauce over the fillets of sole and return to the oven for a further 5 mins.

SOLE SEVILLE PALACE

Preparation time: 50 mins.
About 360 calories/1506 joules
Accompaniments: green salad and potatoes tossed in
butter and parsley

Metric/Imperial

4 soles, each 300g/10 oz,
   cleaned and gutted
juice 1 lemon
salt, white pepper
500ml/6 fl oz water
1x15ml/1 tbs butter
For the sauce:
2 tomatoes
½ red pepper
100g/4 oz mushrooms
25g/1 oz butter or
   margarine
25g/1 oz flour
125ml/4 fl oz fish liquor
125ml/4 fl oz white wine
salt, white pepper
50g/2 oz stuffed green
   olives

American

4 soles, each 10 oz,
   cleaned and gutted
juice 1 lemon
salt, white pepper
2 cups water
1 tbs butter

2 tomatoes
½ red pepper
¼ lb mushrooms
2 tbs butter or
   margarine
2 tbs flour
½ cup fish liquor
½ cup white wine
salt, white pepper
½ cup stuffed olives

Rinse the soles, and pat dry. Sprinkle with a little lemon juice. Cover, and leave for 10 mins. Season with salt and pepper.

Bring the water, with the butter and remaining lemon juice, to the boil and add salt. Poach the soles gently for 10 mins. Remove from the liquor and drain well. Arrange on a heated serving dish, cover, and keep warm. Strain the fish liquor and measure out 125ml/4 fl oz/½ cup.

For the sauce, skin, seed, and chop the tomatoes roughly. Seed the red pepper and slice finely. Slice the mushrooms. Melt the butter or margarine in a saucepan and fry the tomatoes, pepper, and mushrooms for 5 mins. Stir in the flour, and slowly pour in the fish liquor and white wine. Simmer gently for 5 mins. After 3 mins. add sliced olives. Check the seasoning, and pour over the soles.

Sole Seville Palace.

TIP
Prawn sauce tastes very good if you add 1x15ml/ 1 tbs of freshly chopped dill.

SQUID IN TOMATO SAUCE

Preparation time: 1 hr. 25 mins.
About 720 calories/3014 joules
Accompaniments: crusty bread and boiled rice

Metric/Imperial

1½kg/3½ lbs small squid, frozen
2 onions
2 cloves garlic
2 carrots
2 sticks celery
few sprigs parsley
3x15ml/3 tbs olive oil
125ml/4 fl oz white wine
4x15ml/4 tbs tomato purée
250ml/8 fl oz warm water
salt, white pepper

American

3½ lbs small squid, frozen
2 onions
2 cloves garlic
2 carrots
2 sticks celery
few sprigs parsley
3 tbs olive oil
½ cup white wine
4 tbs tomato paste
1 cup warm water
salt, white pepper

If necessary defrost the squid according to instructions on the packet. Remove the transparent backbone and clean the inside. Remove the head and inkbag and pull out the hard core at the centre of the tentacles. Cut off the tentacles and cut into bite-size pieces. Slice the body into rings.

Chop the onions, garlic, carrots, celery, and parsley finely. Heat the oil in a saucepan and cook the vegetables for 2 mins. until lightly coloured. Pour in the white wine and simmer for 5 mins. until the liquid has almost evaporated. Stir in the tomato purée and the water. Season with salt tomd pepper. Add the squid, and poach gently for 45 mins. Pour into a heated serving dish.

SQUID WITH RICE

Preparation time: 1 hr. 15 mins.
About 935 calories/3913 joules

Metric/Imperial	American
1kg/2¼ lbs small squid, frozen	2¼ lbs small squid, frozen
3x15ml/3 tbs olive oil	3 tbs olive oil
2 cloves garlic	2 cloves garlic
salt, white pepper	salt, white pepper
4x15ml/4 tbs brandy	4 tbs brandy
850ml/1½ pints water	3¾ cups water
400g/14 oz long grain rice	1¾ cups long grain rice
50g/2 oz butter	4 tbs butter
50g/2 oz Parmesan cheese, grated	2 tbs Parmesan cheese, grated
parsley for garnish	parsley for garnish

If necessary, defrost the squid according to instructions on the packet. Remove the transparent backbone and clean the inside. Remove the head and inkbag, and pull out the hard core at the centre of the tentacles. Cut off the tentacles and cut into bite-size pieces. Slice the body in rings.

Heat the olive oil in a saucepan. Fry the peeled cloves of garlic for 3 mins. and remove. Add the squid and fry for 5 mins. Season, and pour in the brandy. Cover the pan and simmer for 20 mins. If necessary, add a few tablespoons of water. Boil the rice in salted water for 15 mins. Add the squid to the rice, and continue cooking for 10 mins, stirring frequently, until all the liquid has been absorbed. Stir the butter and Parmesan cheese into the rice. Remove the pan from the heat and leave the contents in it for 5 mins. Then pour into a heated serving dish, and garnish with chopped parsley.

STUFFED SQUID

Calamaretti Imbottiti

Preparation time: 1 hr. 35 mins.
About 470 calories/1967 joules

Metric/Imperial	American
1kg/2¼ lbs small squid, frozen	2¼ lbs small squid, frozen
For the stuffing:	
6 tinned artichoke hearts	6 canned artichoke hearts
4 anchovy fillets	4 anchovy fillets
few sprigs parsley	few sprigs parsley
1 egg	1 egg
50g/2 oz dried breadcrumbs	4 tbs dried breadcrumbs
salt, white pepper	salt, white pepper
In addition:	
25g/1 oz dried Italian mushrooms	2 tbs dried Italian mushrooms
125ml/4 fl oz lukewarm water	½ cup lukewarm water
2 onions	2 onions
2 cloves garlic	2 cloves garlic
1 stick celery	1 stick celery
1 carrot	1 carrot
500g/1 lb tomatoes	1 lb tomatoes
4x15ml/4 tbs olive oil	4 tbs olive oil

If necessary defrost the squid. Remove the tentacles, head, and insides. Pull out the hard core at the centre of the tentacles. Remove the outer skin.

For the stuffing, finely chop the tentacles, artichoke hearts, anchovy fillets, and parsley and place in a bowl. Mix well with the egg and breadcrumbs and season with salt and pepper. Stuff the squid bodies with the mixture, and fasten the openings with wooden cocktail sticks. Soak the mushrooms in lukewarm water. Chop the onions and garlic finely, and the celery and carrot roughly. Skin, seed, and dice the tomatoes.

Heat the olive oil in a shallow, wide ovenproof pan, and fry the squid for 3 mins. Add the onions, garlic, celery, and carrot, and cook for a further 3 mins. Add the mushrooms with their soaking liquid and the tomatoes. Cover the pan and simmer for 45 mins. Serve in the pan.

TIP
When you prepare squid, make sure it is served very hot. Cooled squid often becomes tough.

Stuffed squid: an Italian speciality.

STURGEON KEBABS

Preparation time: 30 mins.
About 220 calories/920 joules

Metric/Imperial	American
For the marinade:	
4x15ml/4 tbs olive oil	4 tbs olive oil
juice 1 lemon	juice 1 lemon
salt, white pepper	salt, white pepper
2½ml/½ tsp paprika	½ tsp paprika
1 onion	1 onion
For the kebabs:	
750g/1½ lbs sturgeon	1½ lbs sturgeon
15 bay leaves	15 bay leaves
250ml/8 fl oz boiling water	1 cup boiling water

The roe of the sturgeon is known all over the world as caviare. There are many kinds of sturgeon. It is the largest ones, which live in the Black Sea and the Caspian Sea, that provide the caviare. Sturgeon meat is mainly from the common sturgeon, which can also be found in the North Sea.

Mix the olive oil with the lemon juice, salt, pepper, and paprika. Chop the onion finely, and add to the marinade. Rinse the sturgeon and cut in 4cm/1½ in. cubes. Place in the marinade, cover, and leave in a cool place for 2 hrs. Turn occasionally.

Place the bay leaves in a bowl and cover with boiling water. Leave to soften. Remove the sturgeon cubes from the marinade, and drain the bay leaves. Thread 4 skewers alternately with fish cubes and bay leaves. Brush with the marinade. Put the kebabs on a grill rack and place under a preheated hot grill. Grill for 3 mins. on all sides, brushing occasionally with the marinade.

Sturgeon kebabs: the delicate flesh is brushed with a tasty marinade and grilled.

Tench Lorraine style are poached before being covered with a creamy sauce and grilled for a short time.   ►

TENCH

The tench, like its cousin the carp, prefers slow running or still waters with muddy bottoms because it is in the mud that it finds most of its food. Tench are also farmed in ponds. The flesh is very flavoursome although, because the fish has lived in muddy waters, it sometimes acquires a musty aftertaste.

Tench can reach a length of 50cm/19½ in. and weigh up to 5kg/11 lbs.

They have a blue-green back and yellowish belly. The body is covered with small scales that should be removed before frying, as the tasty skin can be eaten as well. Tench also taste good when poached.

TENCH LORRAINE STYLE

Preparation time: 1 hr. 10 mins.
About 415 calories/1737 joules
Accompaniments: mixed salad and creamed
mashed potato

Metric/Imperial

4 tench, each 300g/10 oz
juice 1 lemon
salt
few sprigs parsley
1 sprig fresh, or 1 pinch
  dried thyme
25g/1 oz butter
1 small bay leaf
4 white peppercorns
4 onions
125ml/4 fl oz white wine
1x15ml/1 tbs butter
4 shallots
For the sauce:
125ml/4 fl oz fish liquor
125ml/4 fl oz cream
2 egg yolks
50g/2 oz butter
parsley for garnish

American

4 tench, each 10 oz
juice 1 lemon
salt
few sprigs parsley
1 sprig fresh, or 1 pinch
  dried thyme
2 tbs butter
1 small bay leaf
4 white peppercorns
4 onions
½ cup white wine
1 tbs butter
4 shallots

½ cup fish liquor
½ cup cream
2 egg yolks
4 tbs butter
parsley for garnish

Slit open the belly of the tench and gut. Scale the fish and cut off the fins. Rinse inside and out, and pat dry. Sprinkle inside and out with lemon juice. Leave for 15 mins. Season with salt. Chop the parsley and thyme finely. (Crumble dried thyme between your fingers.)

Melt the butter in a shallow saucepan and add the herbs, bay leaf and peppercorns. Slice a piece off the bottom of each of the onions. Place one onion into each fish, cut-side down. Place the tench, with the back facing upwards, in the saucepan. Pour over the white wine and bring to the boil. Cover and poach gently for 15 mins.

Melt the butter in an ovenproof dish. Finely chop the shallots and fry for 5 mins. until transparent. Carefully lift the fish out of the saucepan, drain, and place on top of the shallots. Keep warm. Pour the fish liquor through a sieve into a small saucepan. Reduce to 125ml/4 fl oz/½ cup by boiling rapidly for about 15 mins.

For the sauce, mix the cream with the egg yolks in a bowl. Whisking constantly, pour in the hot fish liquor, and then beat in the butter. Pour the sauce over the tench. Place under a preheated grill for 5 mins. Garnish with parsley.

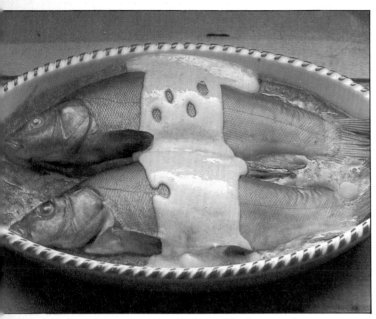

Tench are delicious when baked with cheese and a savoury tomato sauce.

TROUT

Trout has an excellent culinary reputation. Its delicious flesh melts in the mouth.

There are two kinds of freshwater trout, both belonging to the salmon family. One is the brook trout, that lives in cold, clear waters and usually weighs 250-375g/8-12 oz. There have always been brook trout. Not so the second kind, the rainbow trout. This slightly larger, more robust relative has been reared in trout farms since 1880.

There are also sea trout. They can weigh up to 15 kg/33 lbs and are treated like salmon. The following recipes, however, use the small freshwater trout, which is available fresh and frozen. Its fillets are also available smoked.

BAKED TENCH

Preparation time: 60 mins.
About 275 calories/1151 joules

Metric/Imperial	American
4 tench, each 300g/10 oz	4 tench, each 10 oz
juice 1 lemon	juice 1 lemon
salt	salt
500g/1 lb tomatoes	1 lb tomatoes
2 onions	2 onions
25g/1 oz butter	2 tbs butter
salt, white pepper	salt, white pepper
4 slices Emmenthal cheese (100g/4 oz)	4 slices Swiss cheese (¼ lb)

Preheat oven to 200°C/400°F/Gas 6. Slit open the belly of the tench and gut. Scale the fish and cut off the fins. Rinse the tench inside and out, pat dry, and sprinkle inside and out with lemon juice. Leave for 15 mins., then season with salt.

Skin and chop the tomatoes roughly, and dice the onions. Melt the butter in a frying pan, and fry the onions for 5 mins., until transparent. Add the tomatoes and cook for a further 15 mins. over low heat, until nearly all the liquid has evaporated. Season with salt and pepper. Pour the tomato sauce into an ovenproof shallow dish and place the tench on top. Place in the preheated oven on the centre shelf for 10 mins. Then place a slice of cheese on each fish and continue baking for 5 mins.

'BLUE' TROUT

Preparation time: 30 mins.
About 260 calories/1088 joules
Accompaniments: creamed horseradish and new potatoes, tossed in butter and parsley

Metric/Imperial	American
4 fresh or frozen trout, each 250g/8 oz	4 fresh or frozen trout, each ½ lb
salt	salt
250ml/8 fl oz hot vinegar	1 cup hot vinegar
dash of white wine	dash of white wine
For the garnish:	
1 punnet mustard and cress	1 punnet cress
1 lemon	1 lemon
1 tomato	1 tomato

Gut the trout and rinse briefly under cold water. Season lightly with salt. Tie each trout in a ring, i.e., tie head to tail. Place on a dish and slowly pour over the vinegar. The trout should turn blue. Bring a saucepan of water to the boil and add a dash of white wine and 1x5ml/1 tsp salt. Poach the trout gently for 15 mins. until cooked. Lift out of the water, drain, and place on a heated serving plate (which could be lined with linen napkins for greater effect). Garnish with snipped mustard and cress, lemon and tomato wedges, and serve.

TIP
When you prepare trout or any other fish 'blue', be careful not to damage the soft covering of the skin. This, in conjunction with vinegar, causes the blue colouring. For this reason, do not salt the fish as it destroys the outer skin covering.

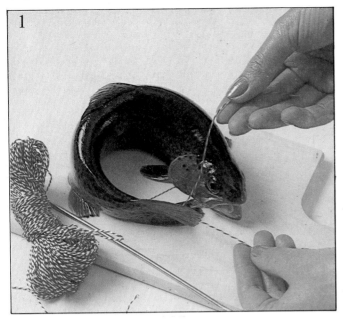

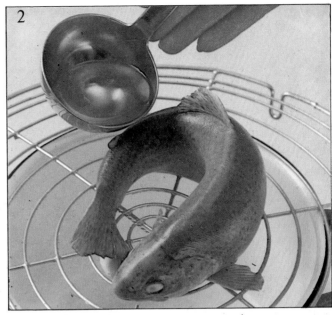

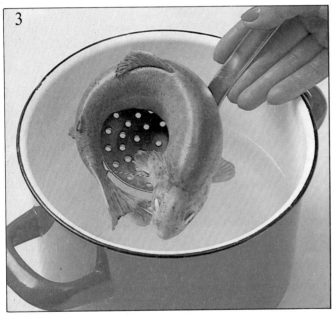

1 *How to make Blue Trout: Before cooking tie the lower jaw to the tail with a piece of string.*

2 *Place the trout on a wire rack and pour over the hot vinegar. This produces the blue colour.*

3 *Bring the water to the boil in a large pan with a teaspoon of salt and a dash of white wine. Slide in the fish, reduce the heat to simmering and poach for 15 mins.*

4 *Carefully lift the poached trout from the liquor with a slotted spoon and drain well. Remove the string and arrange the fish on a serving platter.*

5 *Blue trout is served with sliced lemon, parsley and dill for garnish.*

Stuffed trout: a delicious meal for a very special occasion.

STUFFED TROUT

Preparation time: 1 hr. 25 mins.
About 835 calories/3495 joules

Metric/Imperial

200g/7 oz tinned lobster meat
25g/1 oz butter
2 onions, chopped
1 egg
salt, white pepper
few sprigs each parsley and dill
2x15ml/2 tbs dried breadcrumbs
4 fresh or frozen trout, each 250g/8 oz
juice 1 lemon
2x5ml/2 tsp prepared mustard
butter for greasing
2 small shallots
125ml/4 fl oz Chablis (French wine)
8 puff pastry fleurons
1x15ml/1 tbs butter

American

7 oz canned lobster meat
2 tbs butter
2 onions, chopped
1 egg
salt, white pepper
few sprigs each parsley and dill
2 tbs dried breadcrumbs
4 fresh or frozen trout, each ½ lb
juice 1 lemon
2 tsp hot mustard

butter for greasing
2 small shallots
½ cup Chablis-type wine
8 puff pastry fleurons
1 tbs butter

Preheat oven to 200°C/400°F/Gas 6. For the stuffing, chop the lobster meat, reserving a few red pieces for garnish. Cream the butter in a bowl. Add the chopped onions and the egg. Mix in the lobster meat, salt, and pepper. Chop parsley and dill finely. Add to the mixture with the breadcrumbs, and stir well. Gut the trout, rinse, and pat dry. Season inside and out with lemon juice, salt, and pepper, and spread inside thinly with mustard. Then fill each trout with plenty of the stuffing.

Grease an ovenproof dish with butter. Finely dice the shallots, and sprinkle over the bottom of the dish. Cover with any remaining stuffing. Place the stuffed trout on top, pour in the Chablis, and place in the preheated oven for 30 mins. After 20 mins. place the fleurons in the oven on a piece of foil and heat through. Serve the trout in the dish, garnished with fleurons and the reserved lobster pieces (quickly heated in butter).

TROUT WITH ALMONDS

Preparation time: 40 mins.
About 500 calories/2093 joules

Metric/Imperial	American
4 fresh or frozen trout, each 250g/8 oz	4 fresh or frozen trout, each ½ lb
juice 1 lemon	juice 1 lemon
salt	salt
100g/4 oz butter	½ cup butter
100g/4 oz flaked almonds	⅔ cup flaked almonds
For the garnish:	
2 lemons	2 lemons
parsley	parsley

Rinse the trout and pat dry. Sprinkle the fish inside and out with lemon juice, salt, and pepper.

Melt the butter in a sufficiently large frying pan, and fry the trout first for 1 min. each side, and then for a further 8 min. each side. Add the almonds and fry until golden. Roll the fish in the almonds. Arrange on a heated serving plate, and sprinkle any remaining almonds over the trout. Garnish with slices of lemon and chopped parsley.

TROUT IN RED WINE

Preparation time: 1 hr..
About 350 calories/1465 joules

Metric/Imperial	American
250g/8 oz mushrooms	½ lb mushrooms
1 onion	1 onion
50g/2 oz butter	4 tbs butter
margarine for greasing	margarine for greasing
4 fresh or frozen trout, each 250g/8 oz	4 fresh or frozen trout, each ½ lb
juice 1 lemon	juice 1 lemon
salt, white pepper	salt, white pepper
250ml/8 fl oz red wine	1 cup red wine
1 lemon	1 lemon
25g/1 oz butter	2 tbs butter

A fish speciality: trout with almonds.

Fish cooked in red wine seems quite unusual to us, since we are always told that fish and red wine do not go together. However, you will find that they do mix when you try this famous Swiss recipe.

Preheat oven to 200°C/400°F/Gas 6.

Halve the mushrooms, and chop the onion. Melt the butter in a frying pan and fry the onion until transparent. Add the mushrooms and cook for 3 mins.

Grease an ovenproof dish with margarine. Gut fresh trout, defrost frozen ones, rinse, and pat dry. Sprinkle inside and out with lemon juice, salt, and pepper.

Spread the mushroom mixture on the bottom of the ovenproof dish and cover with the trout. Pour in the wine and place the fish in the preheated oven on the centre shelf for 20 min. Serve immediately, garnished with lemon slices and dots of butter.

TROUT ON MUSHROOMS

Trote sul fondo di champignons

Preparation time: 40 mins.
About 425 calories/1779 joules

Metric/Imperial	American
4 fresh or frozen trout, each 250g/8 oz	4 fresh or frozen trout, each ½ lb
juice 1 lemon	juice 1 lemon
salt, white pepper	salt, white pepper
1x15ml/1 tbs flour	1 tbs flour
4x15ml/4 tbs oil	4 tbs oil
250g/8 oz mushrooms	½ lb mushrooms
butter for greasing	butter for greasing
2x15ml/2 tbs dried breadcrumbs	2 tbs dried breadcrumbs
parsley, chopped	parsley, chopped
25g/1 oz butter	2 tbs butter

Preheat oven to 200°C/400°F/Gas 6. Gut the trout, and rinse inside and out under cold water. Pat dry, and sprinkle inside and out with lemon juice. Season, and roll in flour. Heat the oil in a large frying pan and fry the trout for 2 mins. each side. Keep warm. Trim the mushrooms, and place on the bottom of a greased ovenproof dish. Lay the trout on top. Sprinkle with dried breadcrumbs and chopped parsley, and dot with butter. Place in the preheated oven on the centre shelf for 15 mins.

GRENOBLE TROUT

Preparation time: 50 mins.
About 675 calories/2825 joules

Metric/Imperial	American
4 fresh or frozen trout, each 250g/8 oz	4 fresh or frozen trout, each ½ lb
juice 1 lemon	juice 1 lemon
salt	salt
50g/2oz flour	½ cup flour
125ml/4 fl oz oil	½ cup oil
75g/3 oz butter	⅓ cup butter
50g/2 oz fresh white breadcrumbs	1 cup fresh white breadcrumbs
2x15ml/2 tbs capers	1 tbs capers
For the garnish:	
1 lemon	1 lemon
parsley	parsley

Gut the trout and rinse well under cold water. Pat dry and sprinkle with half the lemon juice. Leave for 5 mins. Season inside and out with salt, and roll in flour.

Heat the oil in a frying pan and fry the fish for 5 mins. each side until golden brown. Remove from the pan, discard the oil, and melt the butter. Replace the trout and fry for a further 5 mins. each side in the butter. Arrange on a heated serving plate. Fry the breadcrumbs in the butter until light brown and sprinkle over the trout. Cover with the remaining lemon juice and the drained capers. Garnish with sliced lemon and parsley sprigs.

Trout on mushrooms: a tasty delicacy from Italy.

Grenoble trout. ➤

Grilled trout.

GRILLED TROUT

Preparation time: 35 mins.
About 540 calories/2260 joules

Metric/Imperial	American
4 fresh or frozen trout, each 250g/8 oz	4 fresh or frozen trout, each ½ lb
juice 1 lemon	juice 1 lemon
4 sprigs parsley	4 sprigs parsley
salt, pepper	salt, pepper
4 sprigs each dill, rosemary, and tarragon	4 sprigs each dill, rosemary, and tarragon
1x15ml/1 tbs flour	1 tbs flour
25g/1 oz butter	2 tbs butter
2x15ml/2 tbs dried breadcrumbs	2 tbs dried breadcrumbs
oil for greasing	oil for greasing
For the sauce:	
100g/4 oz butter	½ cup butter
2x15ml/2 tsp lemon juice	2 tsp lemon juice
few sprigs parsley	few sprigs parsley
1 lemon	1 lemon

TROUT LUGANO STYLE

Trote alla luganese

Preparation time: 1 hr.
About 685 calories/2867 joules

Metric/Imperial	American
50g/2 oz streaky bacon	2 fatty bacon slices
4 tomatoes	4 tomatoes
few sprigs parsley	few sprigs parsley
4x15ml/4 tbs oil	4 tbs oil
salt, pepper	salt, pepper
4 fresh or frozen trout, each 250g/8 oz	4 fresh or frozen trout, each ½ lb
juice ½ lemon	juice ½ lemon
2x15ml/2 tbs flour	2 tbs flour

Dice the bacon, and skin and chop the tomatoes roughly. Chop the parsley.

Heat half the oil in a frying pan and fry the bacon until the fat runs. Add the tomatoes and cook for 5 mins. Season with salt, pepper and parsley. Pour into an ovenproof dish.

Gut the trout, and rinse inside and out. Pat dry and sprinkle with lemon juice. Season with salt and pepper and roll in flour.

Heat the remaining oil in the frying pan and fry the trout for 3 mins. each side. Place on top of the tomatoes and pour the fat over. Cover and cook for a further 10 mins. Serve in the dish.

TIP
Trout are cooked when the eyes protrude, the belly flaps bend outwards, and the fins are easy to pull out.

Gut the trout, wash, and dry. Sprinkle inside and out with lemon juice. Place 1 sprig of parsley in each fish. Leave for 30 mins. to absorb the flavours. Season with salt and pepper. Place 1 sprig each of dill, rosemary, and tarragon in each fish. Roll in flour, cover with melted butter and roll in the breadcrumbs. Line a grill rack with greased aluminium foil and grill the fish for 7 mins. each side.

Meanwhile, for the sauce, melt the butter in a saucepan, remove the white froth that rises to the top, and season with salt and lemon juice. Chop about 5 sprigs of parsley finely and add to the butter. Remove the trout from under the grill, and arrange on a heated serving plate. Garnish with lemon slices and the remaining parsley. Serve the butter separately.

TROUT IN CREAM SAUCE

Preparation time: 35 mins.
About 390 calories/1632 joules
Accompaniments: green salad and buttered new potatoes

Metric/Imperial	American
4 fresh or frozen trout, each 250g/8 oz	4 fresh or frozen trout, each ½ lb
salt	salt
50g/2 oz flour	4 tbs flour
40g/1½ oz butter	3 tbs butter
2x15ml/2 tbs oil	2 tbs oil
100ml/4 fl oz soured cream	½ cup sour cream
parsley for garnish	parsley for garnish

Gut the trout and rinse under cold water. Pat dry, season with salt, and roll in flour.

Melt half the butter and the oil in a large frying pan, and fry the fish for 5 mins. each side. Remove from the pan and arrange on a heated serving plate. Keep warm.

Discard the fat and melt the remaining butter in the pan. Stir in the soured cream and season with salt. Pour over the fish and sprinkle with chopped parsley.

CHINESE FISH

Ten Tjiun yu

Preparation time: 1 hr. 20 mins.
About 530 calories/2219 joules
Accompaniments: boiled rice and soya sauce

Metric/Imperial	American
1 trout, about 400g/14 oz	1 trout, about 14 oz
1 carp, about 1½kg/3½ lbs	1 carp, about 3½ lbs
juice 1 lemon	juice 1 lemon
salt, white pepper	salt, white pepper
50g/2 oz smoked bacon	2 slices smoked bacon
4 large cabbage leaves	4 large cabbage leaves
margarine for greasing	margarine for greasing
500g/1 lb mushrooms	1 lb mushrooms
2 pieces preserved stem ginger	2 pieces preserved stem ginger
3x15ml/3 tbs soya sauce	3 tbs soya sauce
pinch of dried star anise	pinch of dried star anise
250ml/8 fl oz hot water	1 cup hot water
2x5ml/2 tsp cornflour	2 tsp cornstarch
40g/1½ oz pork dripping	3 tbs pork dripping
juice ½ lemon	juice ½ lemon
For the garnish:	
parsley	parsley
1 lemon	1 lemon

Preheat oven to 200°C/400°F/Gas 6. Rinse the trout and carp, gut, and remove membranes from the stomach cavities. Scale the carp, if necessary. Rinse both fish again, and pat dry. Sprinkle inside and out with lemon juice.

Make several cuts across the back of both fish, and rub in plenty of salt and pepper. Cut the bacon in very fine strips and place inside the slashes. Wash the cabbage leaves and pat dry. Grease an oven-proof oval dish with margarine and insert the fish. Slice the mushrooms and ginger finely. Mix and spread over the fish. Sprinkle with soya sauce and star anise. Pour in a little hot water. Cover with a lid or foil and place in the preheated oven on the centre shelf for 30 mins.

During the baking, gradually pour over the remaining water and baste frequently with the juices. Remove from the oven and arrange the fish on top of the cabbage leaves on a heated serving plate. Boil up the juices with a little water and thicken with cornflour. Season, and serve separately.

Heat the pork dripping until smoking and pour over the fish. Sprinkle with lemon juice, and garnish with chopped parsley and sliced lemon.

Chinese fish.

TUNAFISH

The tunafish is one of the largest members of the mackerel family. It is a greedy fish of prey but, at the same time, a kind of gourmet of the sea. It has to be greedy on account of its enormous size: it can weigh up to 500kgs/1102 lbs and reach a length of nearly 3m/10 ft. However, because it chooses its food carefully, the flesh of the tunafish is particularly tasty.

The tunafish likes to feed on herring, and this preference often drives it as far north as the northern North Sea in the summer season. There it is occasionally caught by fishermen—if it has not torn the net and escaped first. The main catch areas, however, are the Mediterranean, the Atlantic coasts of Portugal, the western Atlantic Ocean, and the Pacific Ocean.

The tunafish has a dark blue back, and pink to white flesh, according to the species. It can be cooked or fried like meat, as its flavour is reminiscent of veal.

Tunafish is usually available fresh, preserved in oil or brine, and sometimes smoked. It is an excellent base for salads or sandwiches.

Grilled tunafish.

TROUT NAIROBI

Preparation time: 30 mins.
About 445 calories/1862 joules

Metric/Imperial	American
4 fresh or frozen trout each weighing 250g/8 oz	4 fresh or frozen trout each weighing ½ lb
juice 1 lemon	juice lemon
salt, black pepper	salt, black pepper
2x15ml/2 tbs flour	2 tbs flour
4x15ml/4 tbs oil	4 tbs oil
2 bananas	2 bananas
2x15ml/2 tbs tomato ketchup	2 tbs tomato ketchup
few sprigs parsley	few sprigs parsley
25g/1 oz butter	2 tbs butter

This recipe is named after the town of Nairobi, the capital of Kenya in Africa.

Gut the fresh trout and rinse. Defrost frozen fish. Pat dry and rub inside and out with salt and pepper. Roll in flour. Heat the oil in a large frying pan and fry the trout for 5 mins. each side until golden. Arrange on a heated serving plate. Fry the peeled and halved bananas in the fat remaining in the pan, about 5 mins. Arrange over the trout. Sprinkle with tomato ketchup. Garnish with chopped parsley. Cover with the butter browned in the pan. Serve immediately.

Trout Nairobi.

GRILLED TUNAFISH

Preparation time without marinading: 35 mins.
About 595 calories/2491 joules

Metric/Imperial	American
4 fresh tunafish steaks, each 200g/7 oz	4 fresh tunafish steaks, each 7 oz
1 large onion	1 large onion
few sprigs parsley	few sprigs parsley
For the marinade:	
125ml/4 fl oz olive oil	½ cup olive oil
juice 1 lemon	juice 1 lemon
salt, white pepper	salt, white pepper
In addition:	
1 lemon	1 lemon
125g/4 oz herb butter	½ cup herb butter

Rinse the tunafish briefly and pat dry. Place on a large plate. Cut the onion in very thin slices. Chop the parsley, reserving 2 sprigs for garnish. Cover the fish steaks with the onion slices and chopped parsley.

For the marinade, mix the olive oil with the lemon juice and season with salt and pepper. Pour over the fish, cover, and leave to marinade for 1 hr. Turn after 30 mins.

Drain the tunafish steaks and lay on a grill rack. Grill for 10 mins. each side.

In the meantime, slice the lemon and separate the parsley into small spriglets. Cut the well chilled herb butter in 4 slices.

Arrange the grilled tunafish steaks on heated plates, and place the herb butter on top. Garnish with parsley and lemon slices.

TIP
The tunafish could be rubbed with onion juice before grilling.

TUNAFISH AND SPAGHETTI SALAD

Preparation time without marinading: 50 mins.
About 420 calories/1758 joules

Metric/Imperial	American
For 6 persons	
850ml/1½ pints salted water	3¾ cups salted water
250g/8 oz spaghetti	½ lb spaghetti
375g/12 oz tinned tunafish in oil	¾ lb canned tunafish in oil
3 green peppers	3 green peppers
5 tomatoes	5 tomatoes
3 onions	3 onions
For the marinade:	
100ml/4 fl oz mayonnaise	½ cup mayonnaise
3x15ml/3 tbs milk	3 tbs milk
5 drops of tabasco sauce	5 drops of tabasco sauce
1x15ml/1 tbs soya sauce	1 tbs soya sauce
1x15ml/1 tbs fruit sauce	1 tbs fruit sauce
salt, black pepper	salt, black pepper
1 pinch of sugar	1 pinch of sugar
1x15ml/1 tbs paprika	1 tbs paprika
pinch of chilli powder	pinch of chilli powder
parsley for garnish	parsley for garnish

Boil the salted water in a large saucepan. Break the spaghetti in 4-inch lengths, and boil for 15 mins. Drain and cool. Drain the tunafish, catching the oil in a large bowl. Seed the peppers, and cut in narrow strips. Skin, seed, and dice the tomatoes. Chop the onions.

For the marinade, mix the tunafish oil with mayonnaise, milk, and the tabasco, soya, and fruit sauces. Season with salt, pepper, sugar, paprika, and chilli powder. Break up the tuna flesh with a fork, and add to the marinade with the spaghetti, peppers, onions, and tomatoes. Mix well, cover, and chill in the refrigerator for 30 mins. Serve in a glass bowl, garnished with parsley.

TUNAFISH PROVENÇAL

Preparation time without marinading: 1½ hrs.
About 475 calories/1988 joules

Metric/Imperial	American
750g/1½ lbs tunafish	1½ lbs tunafish
salt, white pepper	salt, white pepper
juice ½ lemon	juice ½ lemon
2x15ml/2 tbs olive oil	2 tbs olive oil
1 sprig each fresh, or ½ tsp each dried, lemon balm, parsley, and thyme	1 sprig each fresh, or ½ tsp each dried, lemon balm, parsley, and thyme
1 onion	1 onion
4x15ml/4 tbs olive oil	4 tbs olive oil
1 clove garlic	1 clove garlic
500g/1 lb tomatoes	1 lb tomatoes
125ml/4 fl oz white wine	½ cup white wine
1x15ml/1 tbs cornflour	1 tbs cornstarch

Preheat oven to 180°C/350°F/Gas 4. Rinse the tunafish, pat dry, and season. Mix the olive oil with lemon juice and pour over the fish. Chop the lemon balm, parsley, and thyme and sprinkle over the fish. Cover and leave to marinade for 1 hr.

Chop the onion. Heat the oil in a casserole and fry the onion and tunafish for 10 mins. Crush the garlic with a little salt. Skin, seed, and chop the tomatoes. Add to the tunafish with the garlic. Cover and simmer for 15 mins. Add the white wine, and place the casserole uncovered in the preheated oven on the centre shelf for 35 mins. Baste frequently with the juices.

Arrange the fish on a heated serving plate. Thicken the cooking juices with cornflour mixed with a little water. Bring quickly to the boil, then pour through strainer over the fish.

NOTE:
In addition, the fish could be larded with anchovy fillets previously soaked in water.

Tunafish provençal is prepared with
plenty of fresh herbs and tomatoes.

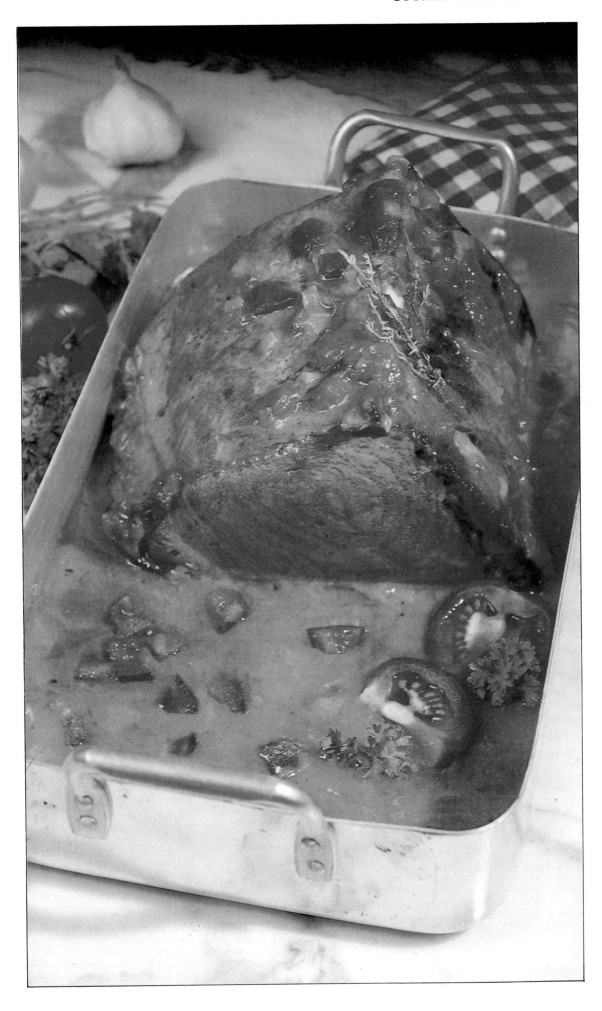

TURBOT

Turbot is one of the largest and finest flat fish and belongs to the sole family. Its smooth body has no scales and it is almost round like a circle. It has a sandy-brown upper skin with bony knobs, and the underside is whitish. Catch areas for turbot are the Mediterranean, and the North and Baltic Seas.

The knobbly skin is usually removed before cooking turbot. The fish can be prepared in many different ways: poached, fried in butter, grilled, or baked with various sauces and stuffings. As the head and bones are quite heavy, you need about 400g/14 oz of whole fish per person.

TURBOT HOTEL BRISTOL

Preparation time: 30 mins.
About 450 calories/1883 joules

Metric/Imperial	American
4 fillets of turbot, each 300g/10 oz	4 fillets of turbot, each 10 oz
juice 1 lemon	juice 1 lemon
8 tinned fillets of anchovy	8 canned fillets of anchovy
100g/4 oz jar stoned green olives	4 oz jar stoned green olives
8 small tomatoes	8 small tomatoes
5x15ml/5 tbs oil	5 tbs oil
salt, white pepper	salt, white pepper
40g/1½ oz herb butter	3 tbs herb butter

Turbot Hotel Bristol.

Rinse the fillets of turbot and pat dry. Sprinkle with lemon juice, cover, and leave to marinade for 15 mins.

Soak the anchovy fillets in a bowl of cold water. Heat the olives with their liquid in a saucepan. Cut off the stalks of the tomatoes and make a cross cut on the top of each. Brush with oil.

Dry the fillets of turbot and place on an oiled grill rack. Place under a preheated grill for 12 mins. Turn the fish halfway through the cooking time. Season, and arrange on a heated serving plate.

Grill the tomatoes for 5 mins. Dry the anchovy fillets and drain the olives. Garnish the fillets of turbot with the anchovy fillets, olives, and tomatoes. Serve the herb butter with the fish or separately.

Turbot Antoinette is served with a delicious cream sauce.

TURBOT ANTOINETTE

Preparation time: 1 hr.
About 585 calories/2448 joules
Accompaniments: lettuce hearts and potatoes tossed in butter and parsley

Metric/Imperial	American
4 turbot steaks, each 300g/10 oz	4 turbot steaks, each 10 oz
juice 1 lemon	juice 1 lemon
For the fish liquor:	
1 onion	1 onion
1.3 litres/2¼ pints water	6 cups water
250ml/8 fl oz white wine	1 cup white wine
salt, 1 bay leaf	salt, 1 bay leaf
12 peppercorns	12 peppercorns
4 lemon wedges	4 lemon wedges
For the cream sauce:	
25g/1 oz butter or margarine	2 tbs butter or margarine
25g/1 oz flour	2 tbs flour
250ml/8 fl oz cream	1 cup cream
salt, white pepper	salt, white pepper
juice ½ lemon	juice ½ lemon
pinch of sugar	pinch of sugar
1x15ml/1 tbs anchovy paste	1 tbs anchovy paste
1x15ml/1 tbs capers	1 tbs capers
100g/4 oz prawns	4 oz shrimps
For the garnish:	
1 lemon	1 lemon
few sprigs parsley	few sprigs parsley

Rinse the turbot steaks well and pat dry. Sprinkle with lemon juice, cover, and leave for 15 mins.

Peel the onion and slice. Put in a wide pan with the water, white wine, salt, bay leaf, peppercorns, and lemon wedges and boil for 5 mins. Add the turbot steaks and poach gently for 20 mins. Remove, cover, and keep warm. Pour the liquor through a strainer.

For the cream sauce, melt the butter or margarine in a saucepan. Stir in the flour and cook for 2 mins. Stirring constantly, pour in 250ml/8 fl oz/1 cup of the strained fish liquor and the cream. Simmer for 5 mins. Season with salt, pepper, lemon juice, and sugar. Add the anchovy paste. With a wire whisk beat the sauce until slightly frothy. Stir in the drained capers and prawns. Heat through but do not boil.

Arrange the turbot steaks on a heated serving plate, and garnish with lemon wedges and parsley sprigs. Serve the sauce separately.

TURBOT DENISE

Preparation time: 50 mins.
About 315 calories/1318 joules

Metric/Imperial

2 fillets of turbot,
  each 300g/10 oz
juice 1 lemon
For the stuffing:
100g/4 oz button
  mushrooms, sliced
25g/1 oz margarine
150g/5 oz poached cod
1 egg yolk
salt, pepper
In addition:
3x15ml/3 tbs white sauce
2 onions
few sprigs parsley
250ml/8 fl oz white wine
1x15ml/1 tbs butter
  for greasing
3x15ml/3 tbs cream
1x5ml/1 tsp paprika
dill for garnish

American

2 fillets of turbot,
  each 10 oz
juice 1 lemon

4 oz mushrooms,
  sliced
2 tbs margarine
5 oz poached cod
1 egg yolk
salt, pepper

3 tbs white sauce
2 onions
few sprigs parsley
1 cup white wine
1 tbs butter
  for greasing
3 tbs cream
1 tsp paprika
dill for garnish

Turbot Denise is usually prepared using whole fish. However, as you can usually only buy huge fish of 1–3kg/2–6 lbs, it is easier to use fillets and stuff them. Sprinkle the fillets of turbot with lemon juice. For the stuffing, fry the sliced mushrooms in hot margarine and cool. Mix well with poached cod flesh, egg yolk, salt, and pepper. Place the turbot skin-side up on a plate and spread with the stuffing (reserve a little for stuffing balls). Roll up and fasten with wooden cocktail sticks. Make a white sauce.

Quarter the onions and place with the parsley in a shallow wide pan. Add the white wine and bring to the boil. Add the fish, cover with buttered grease-proof paper, and poach gently for about 15 mins. Baste occasionally with the liquor. Meanwhile, shape little balls from the remaining stuffing mixture. Add to the pan and poach for about 5 mins.

Remove the fish rolls and stuffing balls, place on a heated serving plate, and keep warm. Strain the fish liquor, and mix with the white sauce and cream. Cook until slightly thickened. Season with paprika. Pour the sauce through a strainer over the fish, and garnish with sprigs of dill.

TIP
If you do not want to bother to make a white sauce, just mix 1x5ml/1 tsp butter with 1x15ml/1 tbs flour and stir into the fish liquor. Bring to the boil and add the cream.

Turbot Denise:
fillets of turbot stuffed with
cod and mushrooms and
served with a white sauce.

Burgenland Zander.

BURGENLAND ZANDER

Preparation time: 55 mins.
About 596 calories/2494 joules

Metric/Imperial

4 fillets of pike-perch,
  each 250g/8 oz
juice ½ lemon
4 fillets of anchovy
salt, paprika
40g/1½ oz flour
40g/1½ oz margarine
2 onions
100g/4 oz streaky bacon
2x15ml/2 tbs tomato purée
250ml/8 fl oz stock
1x15ml/1 tbs butter for
  greasing

American

4 fillets of pike-perch,
  each ½ lb
juice ½ lemon
4 fillets of anchovy
salt, paprika
3 tbs flour
3 tbs margarine
2 onions
¼ lb fatty bacon slices
2 tbs tomato paste
1 cup stock
1 tbs butter for
  greasing

In the Burgenland in Austria, pike-perch is called zander or schill.

Preheat oven to 200°C/499°F/Gas 6.

Wash the fillets of perch-pike and pat dry. Sprinkle with lemon juice. Place 1 fillet of anchovy on each fillet of pike-perch, fold over, and fasten with a wooden cocktail stick. Season with salt and paprika and roll in flour. Melt the margarine in a frying pan, and fry the fish briefly until golden all over. Place in a shallow, ovenproof dish. Finely chop the onions and dice the bacon, and fry until golden. Sprinkle with paprika. Add the tomato purée and pour in the stock. Bring to the boil and pour over the fish. It should be half covered. Cover the dish with buttered greaseproof paper and place in the preheated oven for 25–30 mins.

PIKE-PERCH TAUENTZIEN

Preparation time: 35 mins.
About 395 calories/1653 joules

Metric/Imperial

4 fillets of perch-pike,
　each 200g/7 oz
juice ½ lemon
salt
25g/1 oz butter
250ml/8 fl oz white wine
1 bay leaf
3 cloves
For the sauce:
40g/1½ oz butter
25g/1 oz flour
125ml/4 fl oz white wine
125ml/4 fl oz hot stock
fish liquor
6x15ml/6 tbs cream
parsley and chives

American

4 fillets of perch-pike,
　each 7 oz
juice ½ lemon
salt
2 tbs butter
1 cup white wine
1 bay leaf
3 cloves

3 tbs butter
2 tbs flour
½ cup white wine
½ cup hot stock
fish liquor
6 tbs cream
parsley and chives

Rinse the fillets and pat dry. Sprinkle with lemon juice and salt. Bring the butter and white wine to the boil and add the bay leaf and cloves. Place the fish in the liquor and poach gently for 12 mins.

For the sauce, melt the butter in a saucepan and stir in the flour. Cook for 3 mins. then pour in the white wine and stock. Simmer for 5 mins. Remove the fish from the liquor and arrange on a heated serving plate. Cover and keep warm.

Strain the fish liquor into the sauce. Cook for 3 mins. Remove the pan from the heat and stir in the cream. Chop the parsley finely and snip the chives. Add to the sauce. Heat the sauce until very hot but not boiling, pour over the fish, and serve immediately.

Pike-perch Tauentzien. ➤

STUFFED PIKE-PERCH

Preparation time: 15 mins.
About 570 calories/2386 joules

Metric/Imperial

For the stuffing:
150g/5 oz mushrooms
1 onion
75g/3 oz prawns
40g/1½ oz butter or
　margarine
few sprigs parsley
2x15ml/2 tbs tomato purée
salt, white pepper
In addition:
750g/1½ lbs perch-pike
juice 1 lemon
4 large slices streaky
　bacon
25g/1 oz butter for
　greasing

American

2½ cups mushrooms
1 onion
3 oz shrimps
3 tbs butter or
　margarine
few sprigs parsley
2 tbs tomato paste
salt, white pepper

1½ lbs perch-pike
juice 1 lemon
4 large slices fatty
　bacon
2 tbs butter for
　greasing

Preheat oven to 220°C/425°F/Gas 7. For the stuffing, chop the mushrooms and onion, and prepare the prawns. Melt the butter or margarine in a saucepan. Fry the mushrooms, onion, and prawns, for 10 mins. Chop the parsley and stir into the mixture. Add the tomato purée, and season well with salt and pepper.

Rinse the perch-pike and pat dry. Cut in 4 slices. Sprinkle with lemon juice and spread with a third of the stuffing. Wrap each slice in a slice of bacon, and spread the remaining stuffing on top.

Grease 4 pieces of aluminium foil with butter, and loosely wrap each piece of fish. Place on a baking tray in the preheated oven for 20 mins.

Remove the fish parcels from the oven, unwrap, and arrange fish on a heated serving plate. Pour over the juices and serve.